P9-DET-522

# GARDENING
# PROJECTS
# FOR KIDS

# GARDENING PROJECTS
## *for kids*

### 101 ways to get KIDS outside, DIRTY, and having FUN

**WHITNEY COHEN and JOHN FISHER
OF LIFE LAB**

www.lifelab.org

*Timber Press*
*Portland ∗ London*

Thanks are offered to those who granted permission for use of materials but who are not named individually in the acknowledgments. While every reasonable effort has been made to contact copyright holders and secure permission for elements reproduced in this work, we offer apologies for any instances in which this was not possible and for any inadvertent omissions.

Copyright © 2012 by Whitney Cohen, John Fisher, and Life Lab
Photo credits appear on page 256.
Design by Jody Churchfield
Contents page illustrations by Lorena Siminovich
Sidebar illustrations by Joel Holland

Published in 2012 by Timber Press, Inc.

The Haseltine Building
133 S.W. Second Avenue, Suite 450
Portland, Oregon 97204-3527
timberpress.com

2 The Quadrant
135 Salusbury Road
London NW6 6RJ
timberpress.co.uk

Printed in China

Library of Congress Cataloging-in-Publication Data
Cohen, Whitney.
 The book of gardening projects for kids : 101 ways to get kids outside, dirty, and having fun / Whitney Cohen and John Fisher. -- 1st ed.
    p. cm.
 Includes index.
ISBN 978-1-60469-373-7 (hardcover)
ISBN 978-1-60469-245-7 (paperback)
 1. Gardening. 2. Gardening for children. I. Fisher, John, 1970- II. Title.
 SB457.C63 2012
 635--dc23
                          2011036778
A catalog record for this book is also available from the British Library.

*To our families, and every family that
has come to treasure muddy
footprints, berry patches picked clean,
and all the unexpected delights
of children in the garden.*

# contents

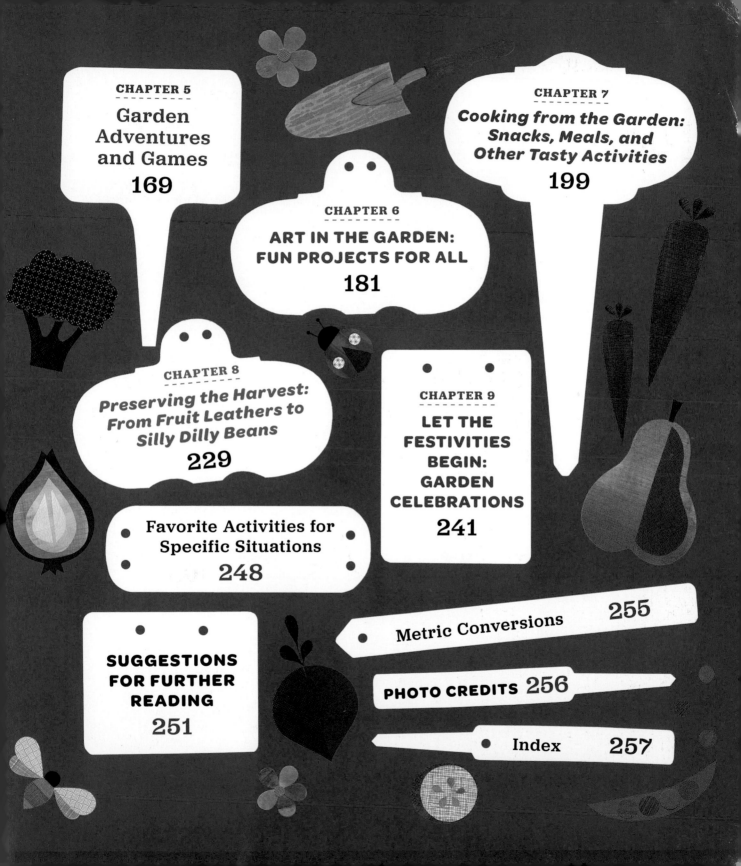

# Acknowledgments

We are so grateful to the many long-standing family gardeners who shared their treasured garden experiences with us. Your traditions, recipes, ideas, and stories inspired us not only as authors, but also as parents. Thank you: Beth Benjamin and Towhee, Tim, Kyla, and Olive Huxley; Sarah Berkowitz and Adam, Charlie, and Kate Underwood; Christof Bernau; Sally, Miles, and Blake Carlile; Amy Carlson and Meg and Greta Lehr; Sharon Danks—Bay Tree Design; Aumar and Jiraum Duryea; Laurel, Alonso, Evan, and Eli Granado; Trish and Lee Hildinger; Stacey, Evan, and Selah Hirscheel; Stacey Kertsman; Matthew Levesque—Building Resources; Tracey Matthes; Kris Nemeth and family; Erika Perloff and Marianna Keel; Caitlin Phillips and family; Kate Purcell—Kate's Kitchen Gardens; Micah Posner and Akiko, Tamarah and Emuna Minami; Paul Simon and family—National Gardening Association; Katie Stagliano and family; Rachael VanLaanen and Scott and Cora Mae Brinton; Deborah, Karsten, Saskia, and Malichi Wade; Donna Wolper; Kim Woodland; and Ama and Sergino Zenya.

Thank you also to our colleagues and supporters at Life Lab and beyond. Specifically, thanks to Abby Bell, Amy Carlson, Ildi Carlisle-Cummins, Juliana Grinvalsky, and Michael Matthews for contributing kid-friendly recipes; Amber Turpin for translating all of the recipes into a common language; Elizabeth Hill for sharing your garden art wisdom and photographs; Abby Bell, Amy Carlson, Gail Harlamoff, Allison O'Sullivan, and Amber Turpin for testing and photographing recipes; and Life Lab interns for testing recipes and creating art projects.

Finally, we want to thank our own families from the bottom of our hearts.

*From Whitney:* Thank you Tod for playing with Nation (not to mention keeping our family garden growing) day after day while I typed away. And to both Tod and Nation, thank you for knowing when to call an end to the typing and insist that I join you outside.

*From John:* Thank you Nadine for supporting my long days and nights on the computer and for letting me sleep in when I needed it. Neli, thanks for putting up with me taking pictures of you constantly when we gardened together.

# PREFACE

*A little gathering here, a little exploration there.*

*Think back.* *Can you remember a natural, outdoor space that held some magic for you? Maybe it was a lake where you discovered the peace of rowing a boat or skipping stones, or a field of tall grass where you played hide-and-seek with friends.*

Over time, all of us discover certain outdoor places where we feel both a sense of peace and the spark of adventure. In these places we feel that we are part of something immense and phenomenal as we remember our connection to the plants and animals, sun and rain, soil, and everything else that makes up the natural world.

Now imagine if you were able to spend time in this place every day, year after year. Envision watching this place grow and change over time, just as you grow and change. What impact would it have on your life? How might this place influence your perspective, your decisions, your sense of yourself and the world?

This is the gift of the family garden. As we harvest vegetables, run through the sprinklers, or gather with friends to celebrate the apple harvest, the family garden is a place where—day after day, year after year—we are reminded of our membership in the intricate web that connects all living things.

## A New Perspective on Gardening

Many gardeners find that once they have children, gardening goes the way of late-night dinner parties and Sunday morning sleep-ins: right out the window. Raising kids and maintaining a garden can be a juggling act and, at times, a family's garden may be forgotten or neglected. In this book, we hope to make it easier for you to merge the garden into your family life, to engage your children in various aspects of your outdoor spaces, and to manage your family garden, no matter its scope or scale.

It may seem counterintuitive, but kids can make great gardening companions. In home gardening, rewards may be measured in basketfuls of strawberries, tomatoes per plant, or even the diameter of the largest pumpkin. Once you involve kids, however, you may start to look for other rewards, such as the frequency with which you hear phrases like, "More kale, please," or "I watered my pea seed every day, and today it is being born!" Your children's love for the outdoors, their sense of connection to plants and animals, and their enthusiasm for fresh fruits and vegetables are the real harvest of a family garden.

## Returning to Our Roots

Picture this. Sonya, age 8, is weeding her pumpkin patch. Out of the corner of her eye, she is surveying the corners of her family garden, looking for the toad she heard croaking last

night. Her mother is pruning a shrub and giving the trimmings to Sonya's 6-year-old brother, who is collecting the big sticks for a fort and adding the small trimmings to their compost pile. Sonya's father is grilling garden-fresh vegetable kabobs for everyone, while her grandmother uses a field guide to identify the bird she sees playing in the birdbath.

For centuries, children and adults have worked together to cultivate the land. In this century, however, the prevalence of large-scale farms and grocery stores has made growing our own food less necessary, and thus less common. Many families, however, are returning to their roots, planting window boxes, patio containers, front yards, backyards, and community

and school gardens. Everywhere you turn these days, from big cities to small towns, you can find families revisiting the longstanding tradition of gardening together. What is behind this resurgence? Why have families started to trade pre-bagged salads and microwave dinners for seeds and trowels?

Whether they are building miniature fairy homes from sticks and leaves or watering their very own tomato plants, kids in a garden have loads of opportunities to explore the outdoors, get physical activity, and gain exposure to fresh, healthy foods. As they see melons growing out of the soil or chickens laying eggs, they begin to recognize that food comes from plants and animals. As they lend a hand in caring for those

Growing your own strawberries can
be pretty thrilling. • Getting back
to the land. • Fun can grow on trees.
The Life Lab Garden Classroom
inspires children and adults.

plants and animals, they develop a sense of connection to the natural world around them. By weaving a garden into family life, parents and kids discover learning opportunities and make memories that will last a lifetime.

We hope to provide a new generation of parents, grandparents, and other family members with the inspiration and information they need to get dirty, plant seeds, and harvest and enjoy the garden's delicious rewards with today's younger green thumbs.

## We're Gardeners, Educators, and Parents

Besides being authors, we are garden education directors at Life Lab, a nonprofit organization in Santa Cruz, California. Founded in 1979, Life Lab's mission is to teach people to care for themselves, each other, and the world through farm- and garden-based programs. We run field trips, day camps, and internships for young people in our Garden Classroom. In a typical Life Lab program, a young person might collect eggs from chickens to make an omelet; harvest roots, stems, leaves, flowers, fruits, and seeds to make a 6-plant-part burrito; or practice job skills by hosting an affordable, organic farm stand in a low-income community.

In addition to our kids' programs, we also train teachers to lead effective garden-based learning programs. Drawing upon decades of Life Lab programs with kids, we have written activity

Co-author Whitney and her son, Nation, tend their front-yard corn patch. • Co-author John and his son, Nell, water on a spring morning.

guides and created workshops for parents and educators interested in bringing learning to life in gardens across the country. Through our work in this field, Life Lab has emerged as a national leader in the garden-based education movement.

After hearing about their kids' experiences in the Garden Classroom, parents started to ask us, "When will you have programs that *we* can attend?" In the last few years, we have created and led camps and garden celebrations for families, inviting parents and kids to come together. The natural joy that we have witnessed in families as they explore and work in the garden together is what inspired us to write this book.

We are also parents. John and his wife, Nadine, have a son named Neli, and Whitney and her husband, Tod, have a boy named Nation. Our expertise in gardening with children comes primarily from many years of working with kids of all ages in the Life Lab Garden Classroom and similar farm- and garden-based learning programs nationwide. Because we both love to be out in our own gardens, we have been overjoyed to discover that our kids love it, too. Nation is still too young for many garden projects, but the garden is one of his favorite places to spend time harvesting sugar snap peas, knocking rocks together, or playing peek-a-boo with the neighborhood cats. John and Neli enjoy cutting chard, making soil soup, hunting for deep red raspberries, and feeding snails to their hens. "More zucchini, please," is music to John's ears.

In addition to our experiences at Life Lab and at home, we have had the great pleasure of visiting and interviewing families who garden together. From Alaska to Vermont, South Carolina to Washington State, we have gathered stories and tips from parents and kids of all ages who enjoy spending time in their gardens together. Whether on the tiny porch of an urban apartment or in a large, open field in a rural town, these families have built lifelong memories in their gardens together. They have also helped us consider very practical tips for making family gardening affordable and attainable, by focusing on activities that require minimal time and preparation and yield maximum fun.

Through our work with children in school gardens and our interviews with active family gardeners, we have discovered a unique method of inspiring kids to develop a deep and lasting connection to a garden. It entails involving your children in meaningful activities at every phase. Toward that end, this book is divided into chapters representing different phases of gardening together as a family, from designing the garden to preparing fresh snacks from the harvest. Within each chapter, you will find activities for engaging kids of all ages.

A garden is always changing, and even the most experienced master gardeners are always discovering new mysteries. As your family and your garden grow together, you and your children will find your own questions to explore. Why are the peas in that corner so much taller than the ones over here? How can we keep that gopher out of our carrot bed? How can we attract more worms into our garden? You don't need to have all the answers, just a willingness to discover alongside your children. Sometimes the best answer a parent can give a child is, "I don't know. Let's find out together!"

Garden time brings everyone together.

# Introduction:

## MAKING GARDENS FUN FOR KIDS

*Home is where the roost is.*

**A**sk your friends about their memories of gardening growing up, and you may hear just about anything. Some adults fondly reminisce about picking persimmons and baking bread with grandparents, others cringe at memories of physical labor, some identify themselves as people with brown thumbs, and others recollect their old vegetable beds with pride. With so many possible outcomes, it is natural to wonder: What if my kids don't like gardening?

Every person is unique and, as all parents know, children are no exception. Some love to get muddy, while others like to stay clean. Some can spend hours (well, okay, kid-hours) playing with dolls in imaginary hideouts, while others would prefer to play tag or hide-and-seek. The best way to make the garden fun for your kids is to consider who they are and then, together with your kids, plan some garden activities, crop plans, and design features that excite them. Here are some tips to consider as you begin to envision your family garden.

## Incorporate Kids' Passions

Some things seem almost universal in their kid appeal, such as building forts, running through sprinklers on a sunny day, joining secret clubs, playing with animals, collecting objects, eating food, and being surprised or grossed out. Find time and space in your garden for some of these passions. Often a very simple idea can capture a child's imagination and make memories that will last for years to come. Here are some examples from families who treasure their gardens.

John and Nadine keep an old cupboard in their garden and, during the growing season, they place a new garden object inside every morning. Neli starts his day with the What's in the Cupboard? game. One of his parents asks the question, and Neli darts outside to find out. It might be a ripe cherry tomato, a chicken feather, or a plastic trowel. The object isn't really so important; the suspense is what Neli loves. Once he has found the object, he and his mom or dad get to talk about it as they look around the garden and see what's growing, what needs water, and what is ready to pick that day.

At Life Lab's Garden Classroom, we have different field trip agendas for different seasons and grade levels. Recognizing the universal appeal of animals, however, we have included a visit with the chickens into every one of our field trips. In addition, acknowledging kids' love of joining clubs and being grossed out, we created the Fear Factor Club for our summer campers. To join, kids must sit still for 10 seconds with a snail on their faces. Even the ones who choose not to join thoroughly enjoy watching others be initiated.

In addition to the tried-and-true kid pleasers, your children will most certainly have their own favorite things. Follow their lead, and you may come up with garden rituals you never could have imagined on your own. When we interviewed young Lee, he reminisced fondly about a favorite hobby when he was about 8: making concoctions that he called Pickle Potions. In his words, "You take a pickle jar with the leftover juice. Then you walk around the garden and add dirt, rocks, leaves, and sticks. Brew in the sun, smell it, then dump it." In another interview, 9-year-old Kyla said that one of her favorite activities was to sit in a tall tree and survey her garden. She also spoke fondly about planting rocks with her 3-year-old sister, Olive. Later, when Olive went inside, Kyla planted plants where the rocks were and brought Olive out to see what "sprouted." Similar stories came from interviews with parents. Erika, mother of two, remembers days on end when her son, Dylan, would occupy himself with water play in the wading pool while her daughter, Mariana, made fairies from flowers. Now teenagers, Mariana still enjoys cutting flowers and decorating her home with bouquets, and Dylan and his girlfriend recently planted their own potato patch.

While few of these activities involve much gardening, they all serve as hooks that will draw your kids into the garden—making it a place they want to call their own, and a place for you and your family to enjoy countless hours together. This is the foundation of a fun family garden.

## Focus on Fun

Your joyful work in the garden is the most likely thing to encourage your kids to join in. Life Lab trainer Trish Hildinger and her family, for example, have created the First Harvest Jig tradition when something comes ripe for the first time. Whoever discovers the first ripe orange, tomato, or snap pea of the season calls the family together to celebrate with a little dance. Simply role model gardening with a joyful attitude and an open mind, and your kids may find it contagious.

This may mean quieting your inner garden expert, so as not to stifle interesting new experiments. If your child brings home a leggy pumpkin plant from school, for instance, the practical gardener in you may be tempted to compost it, knowing that it doesn't look likely to survive. Because of your child's enthusiasm and attachment to the plant, however, you may need to make a point of keeping an open mind and planting it, just in case. Many parents we interviewed made exciting garden discoveries just by doing things with their kids that they never would have tried otherwise.

## Weave the Garden into Your Everyday Lives

There are so many opportunities to connect the garden with our lives. Of course, the most

*Snapdragons and sticky monkey flowers bring a smile.*

*What's water play without a little mud? • The year's first harvest calls for a jig at Trish's house.*

obvious opportunities involve using garden-fresh flowers and produce in your household whenever possible. Have your kids collect cilantro for your salsas, lettuce for salads, or eggs for breakfast. You may want to keep a fresh flower bouquet in your child's room. Your garden can also be a great venue for school and community projects; kids can conduct science fair experiments on plants in the garden, or grow a pumpkin for their local county fair.

At times of the year when the garden is not in production, plants and growing can continue to be a theme in your household. In John's family, Nadine and Neli enjoy dehydrating persimmons, one of the last crops harvested from their neighborhood. John makes sure to include Neli in houseplant watering and has designated one plant as Neli's own jungle plant. Many families comb through seed catalogs in the winter and, every year, order a new and interesting plant

they've never grown before. One family we interviewed also incorporated plants into their family vacations; they have been to most rose and dahlia gardens in Oregon, and the boys fondly recollect their visits to a carnivorous plant nursery and the San Francisco Conservatory of Flowers.

If your garden is full of things your kids love, then it is likely to become a favorite hangout for them and their friends. Kris, who lives in Alaska, said that in the summertime, her family likes to do everything in the yard and garden.

One of the most fun ways to incorporate your garden into your family life is to use it as a site for birthday parties and other important celebrations. We've included a chapter in this book with garden party ideas.

Families often enjoy linking the garden to books or bedtime stories. There are many great garden-themed children's books available. To find an extensive list of award-winning children's

# KATiE'S KROPS:
## helping feed the hungry

**WHILE SOME KIDS** are wild about teen idols, video games, or dinosaurs, Katie Stagliano is passionate about feeding the hungry. When she was in the third grade, Katie was given a tiny cabbage seedling in school. She planted it in her backyard, and tended it carefully. Over time, Katie's cabbage plant grew so large that passersby would stop to check on it. When a neighbor mentioned the danger of a deer getting to it, Katie's grandfather helped her build a cage around it. When Katie finally harvested her cabbage, it was 40 pounds! While it was growing, Katie and others in her family (who were not especially interested in gardening at the time) discussed what they could do with it. One night at the dinner table, Katie suggested that they share it with people in need. She and her mother called a local soup kitchen where their generosity was met with just the enthusiasm needed. They delivered the cabbage and stayed to help serve it in a soup that fed 275 people.

Katie was hooked, and has been growing food to feed the hungry ever since. By the time she was 12, she was overseeing eight gardens, located at homeless shelters, friends' houses, in a neighborhood garden, and at the homes of people who supported her cause. She and her friends and family plant the gardens, and each site has

*After growing a giant cabbage that fed 275 people, Katie Stagliano started Katie's Krops.*

volunteers to maintain them. Ultimately, all the produce is donated to local soup kitchens. Last year, they donated about 2,000 pounds of fresh vegetables. Katie and her family have started their own nonprofit, called Katie's Krops (katieskrops.com), and Katie hopes, one day, to have at least a garden in every state and to inspire as many kids as possible to garden. Describing the impact of this project on Katie's life, Stacy Stagliano, her mother, said, "It has changed Katie's life 100 percent. It has opened her eyes to the world. She realizes that there are kids just like her who are homeless, and she can do something to make a difference. It also opened her eyes to a world of people who step up to support kids. She's now confident speaking in front of people. There isn't anything Katie can't do."

The organization has also influenced Katie's entire family and community. Katie's backyard is full of edible crops, and they compost their food scraps. Stacy traded in her car for a truck to haul everything, and their family travel is tied in with Katie's speaking schedule. Even Katie's school has incorporated their school garden into all subject areas. In Stacy's words, "Every single aspect of our lives has been touched."

Katie summarizes what she's learned: "The people we donate food to are just like you and me, but they had a bad situation. Maybe their house caught on fire or they couldn't pay their medical bills. Something happens to them and they're unable to buy enough food. Donating food to soup kitchens is the most rewarding part of what I do because I actually get to see where the produce is going."

*During the summer at Kris's home in Alaska, the garden becomes the family room. • Making dried persimmons for a winter garden treat. • Gardens make for great birthday parties and more.*

books with garden themes, look for the winners of the American Horticultural Society's Growing Good Kids—Excellence in Literature Book Awards. We've also included some favorites in Suggestions for Further Reading, at the end of this book.

By incorporating your kids' passions into the garden, focusing more on fun and enjoyment than on flawless yields, and weaving the garden into other aspects of your children's lives, you are setting the stage for raising a new generation of garden-lovers.

Fishing for fun in a garden pond.

**Chapter 1**

# DESIGNING A Play-Friendly GARDEN

SNEAK PEEK: Add whimsy and a bit of magic • Make the most of small spaces • Save time and effort • and more

*Sharon's yard is a masterful mix of year-round edible treats.*

A family garden will look and feel very different from a typical adult garden. You may have racetracks for toy cars encircling your tomato plants, miniature dinosaurs creeping through your lettuce beds, or plants from spilled seeds sprouting in the middle of pathways. These are all signs that you are on the right track to making your garden a magical world for your children, a place where they can imagine, explore, play, and dream.

Whether you are designing a new garden or making an existing garden more family friendly, here are some rules of thumb:

- Involve your kids in the garden design
- Make your garden play-friendly
- Create a garden that's as safe as it is fun
- Add whimsy and a bit of magic

- Make the most of small spaces
- Create a welcoming outdoor gathering area
- Use ideas that save time and effort

## *Involve Your Kids in the Garden Design*

Talk to kids who love their gardens, and you will often hear about things you might never have considered part of a garden before, like catapults, painting easels, sand boxes, Frisbee targets, or gopher-viewing chambers. Kids are more likely to feel ownership of the garden, and to enjoy spending time there, if they can see themselves reflected in the planning and design. Of course, the best way to achieve this is to involve them every step of the way.

Whether you are installing a new garden or revamping an existing one, consider going to other gardens together and making notes of what you and your kids like best. You can then involve them in brainstorming and mapping appealing garden elements.

It should come as no surprise that some of the best kid-friendly garden design ideas have come from kids themselves. Lee, a spirited 10-year-old, suggested to his mom and dad that they build a ship's crow's nest in their garden. And so, right in the center of their suburban backyard, they have a tall perch from which Lee can survey the neighborhood.

Some less elaborate but equally whimsical kids' ideas include child-sized nests made from woven branches, moats or miniature rivers for floating leaf boats, and outdoor sitting areas for favorite dolls.

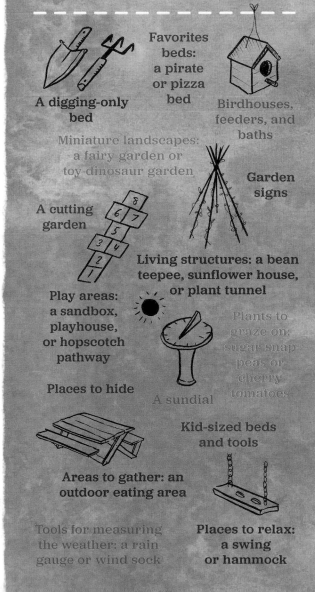

# A FEW FUN FAMILY GARDEN FEATURES

We visited many family gardens while writing this book, and came across wonderful ideas. Here are just a few to play with as you begin your own:

A digging-only bed

Favorites beds: a pirate or pizza bed

Birdhouses, feeders, and baths

Miniature landscapes: a fairy garden or toy-dinosaur garden

Garden signs

A cutting garden

Play areas: a sandbox, playhouse, or hopscotch pathway

Living structures: a bean teepee, sunflower house, or plant tunnel

Places to hide

A sundial

Plants to graze on: sugar snap peas or cherry tomatoes

Areas to gather: an outdoor eating area

Kid-sized beds and tools

Tools for measuring the weather: a rain gauge or wind sock

Places to relax: a swing or hammock

*Trish and Lee on the lookout for garden fun.
• Surf's up–in the form of a swing, along
with a driftwood-carved see-saw and wine
barrel playhouse. • The swinging boat in this
shade garden holds the whole family.*

## Make Your Garden Play-Friendly

Family gardening isn't just about growing and tending to plants. Of course we want our children to have those experiences and gain those life skills, but if that's all you focus on, your child may soon lose interest. One of a child's main jobs in life is to explore and play, and most kids are really good at it. Creating a garden that meets your needs and those of your child is a great goal. Many parents we talked to attribute their love for gardening to the time they spent playing, eating, relaxing, or having adventures in their parents'

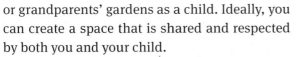

or grandparents' gardens as a child. Ideally, you can create a space that is shared and respected by both you and your child.

Seeing balls and bikes lying in a bed of new transplants will frustrate any gardener. On the other hand, we do not want our kids to feel they have to tiptoe around the garden. In order to make your garden both playful *and* productive, it is important to discuss the boundaries of vulnerable growing areas and play spaces. This might just entail reminding your child how fragile seedlings are but, if needed, you can create barriers and borders with fencing, recycled lumber, branches, bricks, stones, or urbanite. Many families with very young children find that creating a border prevents young ones from picking unripe berries and fruit. As children grow older, parents are able to open these spaces back up and teach their kids to identify and pick only ripe fruit.

In a family garden, paths should be wide and beds narrow so that kids can wander easily between the beds. A nice way to mark out new beds is to have two kids stand facing each other with their arms stretched in front of them. Have them touch fingertips and measure the distance between them. This will give you a rough measurement for a bed width that will allow your children to reach the center without stepping on the bed itself.

If you have a fair amount of yard space, keep your most vulnerable plants as far as possible from the play areas, and surround play areas with plants that can withstand some day-to-day trampling by feet, bikes, balls and the like. Some hardy examples include flowering shrubs, woody perennials, sedums, and groundcovers. Regardless of

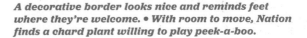

*A decorative border looks nice and reminds feet where they're welcome. • With room to move, Nation finds a chard plant willing to play peek-a-boo.*

# WATCH THE GARDEN, NOT THE TV

*Sharon created an irresistible way to enter the garden.*

**SHARON DANKS,** mother of two and environmental planner at Bay Tree Design Inc., has designed her family's garden to feed the whole child, and not just with veggies. Having a diverse garden where her daughters can explore, hide out, and manipulate the environment serves to keep her children engaged when she sends them out to watch the garden. Sharon leaves tree prunings in her yard and cuts long plum tree branches to build forts. She uses bamboo to build teepees and support hiding places inside tomato forests, and she encourages her kids to carve out spaces in the garden that they can call their own.

Admittedly there are elements of potential risk in her yard: thorns, boulders to jump from, two small ponds, retaining wall drop-offs, and a steep slide on a hillside– but these and other features can help kids develop a command of their environment. Her garden leads to creativity, exploration, real experiences, and negotiating the world with a physical perspective, all of which can be hard to come by in a suburban setting. When her kids are done exploring, they turn to snacking, settling down in their garden hideaways with some "weed-os"–sorrel leaves filled with edible berries and weeds, and other tasty treats that ripen each season.

*So much dirt, so little time. Rocks are fun. • Bigger is better for staying out of small mouths.*

space, almost all of the parents we talked to mentioned the importance of having a digging-only bed for their young children. In a digging-only bed, there are no plants, just shovels and soil—and maybe a toy dump truck or two. This garden bed is like a sandbox at the park where kids might play with toys, plant twigs, or just dig big holes. Some kids told us they remember carving rivers and floating boats in their garden beds, and others described making mud baths and body paint pits. As parents with small kids, we have found that having a dirt play area keeps our kids and their friends engaged until dark, which we welcome gladly while tending to other garden tasks.

## Create a Garden that's as Safe as It is Fun

Gardens are relatively benign spaces, but there are a few things to keep in mind so everyone stays safe and sound. Be sure to test your soil for lead. Lead contamination can come from soil that is imported from a contaminated source or from lead paint, which was common in pre-1970 paint formulas. Lead paint chips and leaching can contaminate soil. If you are gardening in a new site, especially in an urban setting, take the time to test your soil. Confer with your local environmental health office or nursery center for testing resources, or mail a sample to a testing service, such as the Soil and Plant Tissue Testing Laboratory at the University of Massachusetts, Amherst (umass.edu/soiltest) in the U.S., the University of Guelph Laboratory in Ontario, Canada (guelphlabservices.com), or the Royal Horticulture Societies Soil Analysis Service in the United Kingdom (rhs.org.uk). If your soil is contaminated, you will need to remove and replace it, or garden in above-ground raised beds that are protected from the original soil and filled with imported soil.

Chemical fertilizers, weed killers and insecticides are often potent toxins and we don't believe they are worth having around your family garden. Humans have been growing food for thousands of years without chemicals, and you can too. Start with healthy soil that can be amended with nature's fertilizer—compost. Practice organic gardening methods, and if you feel the need to turn to a pesticide, ask your nursery professional for the least toxic option.

There are tasks and chores that are more suitable to children of specific ages. Keep tasks aligned with your child's abilities and stay close as they take on new skills. Having a child-sized tool that is appropriate for the task can go a long way towards making gardening more manageable. These smaller tools allow kids to dig in alongside you, and give them a sense that the garden is, indeed, theirs as well. A small shovel, watering can, and gloves are sufficient. A mini wheelbarrow, rake, or other tools make nice additions.

We discovered the perfect implement for the job when John sought out a small lightweight pair of hand shears for Neli to cut flowers. John showed Neli how to hold and lock the shears and then they practiced cutting houseplants. Neli takes pride in his tool, which has his name written on it, and he now asks to garden more often than before.

Water in the form of hoses, sprinklers, and watering cans can bring hours of giggles in the yard, but standing water in ponds and containers poses concerns for babies and toddlers. Take care not to allow little ones to access ponds or even buckets, as they can be drowning hazards.

Fences are a good option to create a barrier until your babe is older. We have seen parents design ponds with a sturdy metal grid or a piece of thick plexiglas cut to the shape of the pond and affixed a few inches below the water line. This keeps little ones from falling all the way in and works to support potted water plants.

Mosquitoes are another hazard from standing water, so remove stagnant water from any vessels in your garden. If you have self-contained ponds, consider adding mosquito fish (*Gambusia*). But take care in introducing *Gambusia* where they might enter the surrounding waterways. They have been known to destroy native fish and frog populations in wild settings.

*Gesundheit!* Not all plants are friendly. Allergies and toxic plants can make being outdoors less than enjoyable. Use your best judgment when working with a child that has allergies to plants, and remember that allergic reactions come and go as people age. Seek professional advice for those suffering from allergies.

Poisonous plants are numerous and their toxicities can range from causing minor irritation to death. Different regions have their own species, and people's reactions to baneful bushes vary. Most plant guides note which species and plant parts are toxic, but children don't often confer with these books. Teach your child that not all plants are good for eating and identify the noxious ones when you see them. When we designed the Garden Classroom, we often referred to *Plants for Play* by Robin C. Moore, which is an extensive resource of plants suitable for children's play spaces, and includes a detailed list of noxious plants.

*A tool for everyone, and everyone with their tool. • Practice makes perfect when using new tools.*

# SOME LANDSCAPING PLANTS THAT HAVE TOXIC PROPERTIES

**bleeding heart:** *leaves and roots*
**bulbs:** including daffodils, narcissus, hyacinths, snowdrop, and others
**caladium castor bean:** *seeds*
**English ivy:** *leaves and berries*
**euphorbia:** *sap*
**foxglove:** *leaves and seeds*
**hydrangea:** *bulbs, leaves, and branches*
**iris:** *stems and rhizomes*
**larkspur**
**lily of the valley:** *leaves and flowers*
**monkshood:** *especially the berries*
**oleander**
**poinsettia**
**rhubarb:** *leaves*
**rhododendron**
**yew berries**

*Daffodils are toxic when ingested, but Neli knows bouquets aren't for tasting.*

## Add Whimsy and a Bit of Magic

Family gardens should be whimsical spaces. Some gardens contain play areas similar to those found in any other yard: a sandbox, a playhouse, or a plastic pool, to name a few. These work well to keep your child engaged in the yard while you get down and dirty. Kate Purcell, a garden designer from Kate's Kitchen Gardens, helped install a hopscotch pathway in one of her gardens. She suggests using fancy flagstone to disguise it in a formal path, or using handmade stepping stones, log rounds, or recycled items set in a pathway made of tumbled glass, beach stones, or decomposed granite for a more light-hearted feel. She has seen that having something to get kids out and interested in the garden is often all it takes. The promise of play and a child's imagination make a great duo.

Other design features are more plant-oriented, and equally exciting for kids, such as bean teepees and sunflower houses. Often, by simply tweaking the scale you can make a typical garden feature exciting to kids. One father we talked to was growing a pumpkin jungle, with plants packed tightly together. His children liked to climb through it, hide behind big leaves, and pretend to be dinosaurs. Other parents create miniature landscapes where their children build fairy homes or play with small dolls. Still other families choose plants based on their kids' favorite things. When we talked with Trish and Lee, for example, they were in the process of planting a pirate bed in their garden, just beneath the crow's nest. Other favorites beds include rainbow beds, with flowers for

Rope plus tree equals instant fun.

# WHAT'S YOUR sign? LABELING GARDEN SPOTS

Sign design and materials are limited only by your imagination. Here are some creative sign ideas we've seen.

big wooden spoons
rubber stamped stones
cut-up vertical blinds
etched giant zucchini
painted plexiglass scraps

Kids like making their mark in the garden.

every color of the rainbow (sometimes even in the shape of a rainbow); zoo beds, where all of the plants have animal names (like tiger lilies and lamb's ear); and pizza beds, where you can grow wheat, tomatoes, herbs, and other ingredients for making pizza. When kids make signs for their garden beds, they feel an increased sense of ownership over what they have planted, and they also remember what they have to look forward to throughout the growing months.

# FEEDING Two Birds WITH One Seed: FAIRY-TALE FARM

*Fairy-Tale Farm fills a double backyard, thanks to creative thinking.*

**WE CAME ACROSS** many suburban neighbors with a gate or portal connecting each other's yards, but this relationship stood out from the rest. Fairy-Tale Farm is a backyard oasis made up of two suburban yards located in a densely packed residential area.

When the small house next door went up for sale, homeowners Deborah and Karsten were concerned that it would be developed into another set of three-story townhomes overlooking their own one-story home and yard. Micah and Akiko were interested in buying the house, but they could only afford to do so if they built a rental unit in the back. The couples worked together to find a solution that met both of their needs. Through a legal agreement, Deborah and Karsten purchased 33 percent of the property, allowing Micah and Akiko to afford their dream of owning a home. The finances worked so that no rental unit was needed, and they were able to keep both backyards open for gardening and more. The fairy tale doesn't end here. Each family has two young daughters, and they all enjoy gardening and community building. Over years of being neighbors, the families have transformed their adjoining backyards into something much more than a family garden. They have removed the fences between their yards and added a large hen house, beehive, and a dining table in the center of the garden. They host monthly events such as DIY (do-it-yourself) farmers' markets, live music and dancing, dinners prepared by ex-chef Karsten, and drawing classes, making this family garden a community garden. Deborah's family does the bulk of the gardening, so when Micah's family harvests, they pay a dollar per item to keep it all even.

Many parents use gardens as places to engage their children with the great outdoors. What better place, for example, to take up bird watching, discover the sun's changing angles, or experience weather through the seasons? Toward this end, many families have incorporated bird feeders or baths, sundials, rain gauges, and other tools into their gardens for observing and measuring natural phenomena. By adding hammocks and swings, and creating areas for reading and relaxing, families further encourage their kids to head outside, if simply to hang out and enjoy themselves.

If there is an area in the garden where your kids spend a lot of time, whether it is a swing set or a pumpkin jungle, consider lining the pathway with plants for grazing. A mother and gardener we talked to lined the pathway to the play structure in her garden with strawberries, mints, lemon verbena, and grapevines. At Life Lab, we

*Playhouse time gives baby plants a chance to grow and allows kids to be outside on rainy days.*

1

Who can resist a
bean teepee?

have a row of nectar suckers on the way to the kitchen and kids love to stop and pick flowers to drink from. Examples of great nectar suckers include salvias with big, tube-like flowers, such as *Salvia karwinskii* (hummingbird sage) and *Phlomis fruticosa* (Jerusalem sage), as well as honeysuckle, passion flower, and trumpet vine.

By placing food-foraging plants along pathways, you can ensure that kids will have plentiful opportunities to harvest and enjoy some fresh produce from their garden. Select plants that ripen at various times through the year, and you can encourage healthy snacking throughout the seasons.

## Creating Garden Hideaways

Before we built the Garden Classroom at Life Lab, we asked children to draw maps of their dream gardens. In addition to some of the more wild ideas (including a helicopter landing pad), almost every child included a place to hide. Kids just love cubbies, caves, secret passages, and hideaways. In a garden, these spaces often occur naturally, under the hanging branches of a tree or behind a row of blueberry bushes. Others are created intentionally, as in the case of tree houses or clubhouses inside flower domes. Trish and her neighbors, for example, built a hobbit hole, where their kids can travel back and forth between their yards.

*A hobbit-sized door. Everyone wants to know what's on the other side.*

# The GARDEN as a REPURPOSING Mecca

*A favorite of Matthew's grandson, this rain catcher is made from coils salvaged from a vending machine.*

**MATTHEW LEVESQUE** is the director of San Francisco nonprofit Building Resources. A master of reusing materials for garden form and function, Matthew has shared his creativity and sense of wonder with his children, and it has trickled down to his grandson, who is fascinated with water. The youngster is especially fascinated by the spiral rain catcher made from giant springs salvaged from a spent vending machine. If there is no rain, he fills the gutters to see the water shimmer and drip down the springs.

With his kids out of the house, Matthew turns to neighboring middle-school-aged students to help with projects, like laying out mosaic floors of scrap marble and granite. "I have never found a kid who can't do it, it is like making a big puzzle. They stay involved till it is done and they always remember the parts that they put in the ground." Of course, most anything you need for your garden design can be purchased immediately at the local home retail store, but stretching your child's imagination and searching for the perfect repurposed trellis, or making an unconventional wind chime from thrift store gems can bring more value and ownership to your family's garden.

It was surprising, in fact, how many of the gardens we visited had pathways into their neighbors' yards. We began to wonder if family gardens were especially enticing to neighbors. Perhaps the joyful squeals, the bright petals of the tallest sunflowers, and the sweet smells of the herbs travel over fences and entice neighbors to join in the fun. Or perhaps it was a coincidence. Regardless, by sharing backyards, many families have found more space for growing a larger variety of foods and flowers, increased opportunities for their kids to play together, and more excuses to gather and enjoy one another's company.

## *Make the Most of Small Spaces*

Not everyone has acres out back to serve as their home garden. But even when your back 40 is 40 square feet, a lot of gardening can be had. For areas not suitable or large enough for garden beds, containers are a great option. Half wine barrels, small wooden planter boxes, ceramic pots, and reused large plastic plant containers all work for planting. Just make sure the container you are using has drainage holes, and that you pay extra attention to watering and fertilizing since the plant will be dependent upon limited resources. If edibles are not a priority, succulent plants like cacti and sedums are great options for containers since they are very drought tolerant. Succulents come in all shapes and sizes. They are hardy, withstanding even the roughest of kids, and they look great with toy dinosaurs or fairies standing amongst them. There are many herbs and flowers suitable for container growing, and some vegetable varieties are specially bred for compactness. While we wouldn't

suggest planting an orchard of trees in individual containers, you can find fruit trees with dwarfing rootstocks, which keep the tree small and suitable for containers. Mulching container plants is a good idea to retain moisture. Straw works well and gravel and stones are a nice addition in an ornamental arrangement. Consult your nursery professional for appropriate plants and corresponding planting mixes for container growing in your region, and don't let lack of space keep your creative gardening mojo from flowing.

We both have small yards and have had to come up with creative ways to fit in all of the gardening we want to do. Whitney's backyard is too shady for many edible plants to grow, so she uses this area for shade-tolerant perennials, gathering areas, and compost. But that doesn't stop her from growing veggies. She just does it in her front yard, where the lawn has been removed and replaced with a couple garden boxes for vegetables, blueberries in containers, perennial pineapple guava plants, and a variety of flowers. John's yard is even smaller, but with careful planning, dwarfing rootstocks, espalier tree training, and summer pruning, he has packed in 15 fruit trees, veggies, a cutting garden, a chicken coop that doubles as a compost pile, and some open spaces for Neli to dig, swing, and draw chalk art. Where there's a will, there's a way—gardeners can always find space to grow something.

## *Create a Welcoming Outdoor Gathering Area*

In our homes we have living rooms, dining rooms, and other areas meant for specific types of gatherings. A family garden can be one of these spaces

*Containers of succulents make for great playscapes.*

as well. Long-time Life Lab employee and friend Erika Perloff has a small house, which seemed a perfect excuse to have her home extend into the garden. Over the years she has created many rooms in her large outdoor space, enhanced by sunflower houses, bean teepees, plant tunnels, and a table and chairs for dining. She designed her garden to come up right next to her house, as if her house were just another room in her garden. From inside her house, window views of bird feeders and baths remind her family that they are surrounded by the garden. Over the years, her family has become accustomed to outdoor living and dining.

Some yards have elaborate outdoor living areas with patio decks, furniture sets, and cooking areas. But not all of us have large yards or the budget to make this feasible. It doesn't have to be all or nothing. Setting aside a space for a table and bench or a few tree stump stools in the middle of a pumpkin patch invites your family to enjoy the garden from a different perspective. A barbeque or fire pit draws us together through primal cues of food and fire, and a simple shade structure or umbrella brings us together for summertime naps or enjoying a book. Create an outdoor space where you can just sit down and enjoy the view. Soon enough your children will be asking you to dine out (in the garden) more often.

## Use Ideas that Save Time and Effort

With soccer games, homework, play dates, and more, life can surely get in the way of family

*Chicken coop, lettuce box, raspberries, and espalier apples— all in 40 square feet.*

gardening. Everyone prioritizes their tasks differently, but we have tried to make gardening less of a burden and more carefree.

In Whitney's garden, her raised, wooden planting boxes have gopher wire installed on the bottom so she can avoid dealing with furry, big-toothed critters. While balancing a job and caring for a young child, she sometimes finds purchasing veggie starts more manageable than growing all of her own transplants. With successive planted crops like lettuce and spinach, Whitney has spaced her transplants farther apart than usual and planted seeds for the same plant in between. This allows her to plant the second succession direct from seed at the same time as the first transplanted succession. The seeded crop is on its way to being harvest-ready around the same time the transplanted crop is being enjoyed in her kitchen. Another trick to planting once for successive harvests is to plant varieties with different growing schedules all at the same time. For example, try planting carrots with a shorter growing span like *Daucus carota* 'YaYa' (58 days to harvest) and a slower growing variety like *D. carota* 'Deep Purple' (80 days to harvest) at the same time, to extend the gathering season. Potatoes are another good plant for this technique, because varieties are usually characterized by early (60–90 days), mid (90–110 days), or late (110–135 days) season. By planting all three at once, you can extend the harvest.

Bean and pea plant varieties present another time-saving option. Beans come in pole and bush varieties and some pea varieties need no support. You can save time and eliminate the need to create, maintain, and store trellising by planting bush beans rather than pole beans. On the other hand, if you have a child ripe for the job of building a trellis or teepee, by all means let them have a go at it and grow those scarlet runner beans.

What you put in your garden, and where, can often save time. Smart and efficient planning is something that comes from observing each year spent in the garden, but you don't have to wait years. For example, to make composting kitchen scraps easier, keep your compost pile close to your kitchen. Parents Guillermo and Amber appreciate the convenience of having their hens adjacent to their kitchen window. When they cook, they are able to toss scraps out their window to their feathered girls. And the chickens get even their 3-year-old son excited about the chore of taking out the compost.

*This kid-sized bench made by Greta's grandpa is perfect for a garden-side read.*

# GARDEN VOLUNTEERS:
## CROPS THAT KEEP ON GIVING

We highly recommend planting reseeding annuals in your garden. If you let them go to seed, you will most likely see them show up as volunteers the next season. You can even spread their seed heads around to other spots in the yard. Here are some popular garden volunteers.

**CUTTING GARDEN FLOWERS:**
amaranth, bachelor buttons, cosmos, fever few, marigolds, nigella, poppies, snap dragons, sunflowers, sweet peas, and zinnias

**EDIBLE FLOWERS:**
borage, calendula, nasturtiums, violas

**OTHER EDIBLES:**
beans, chard, cilantro, dill, fennel, kale, mustard greens, orach

**Note:** *While squash family crops like pumpkins often volunteer, the fruits that develop will most likely be mutants made from cross pollination of different varieties. If you have space in your garden, try growing a few mutant volunteers because they are fun to talk about, and create a bit of anticipation as you watch what develops. Don't, however, count on these for your edible crop because they may or may not have a very good taste or texture.*

Selecting the right place for your plants can also save time and keep your family more involved in the garden. Kitchen gardens by definition grow items used for cooking, and it is beneficial to place those plants in an area that's easy to access. Herbs, greens, and bunching onions are examples of crops that are great to have available for easy snipping. The same concept is true for planting a kids' snacking garden. By having cherry tomatoes, snap beans, peas, lemon cucumbers, berries, and such close to your home, rather than buried deep in the garden, you'll help your kids stay interested in the garden as crops come into maturity. During our spring and fall raspberry harvest windows, it sure is easier to get Neli out of the house and off to wherever we are going by telling him to wait by the berry patch near the door. Edible perennials like berries, asparagus, rhubarb (kids love sour stuff), artichokes, fruit trees, tree kale and collards, and fruiting shrubs like edible currants can keep your garden tasty even when times get too busy for tending to annuals.

It takes a lot of time to water a garden well. While kids love to water, they are not usually the most effective irrigators. That's why John opts for a drip irrigation system with a timer. John finds watering by hand relaxing, but not when he is rushing to work and trying to make sure everything is watered on a 90-degree day. Additionally, drip irrigation saves water and delivers water only where you need it, whereas overhead watering can end up watering your paths and weeds. Save the task of watering the garden for a hot day when water play can be added to the chore. An oscillator or hose with a fan attachment makes for endless play and your garden or lawn will get drenched.

With so many weeds and so little time, mulch can be a great help. Mulching is a very kid-friendly task, and when placed around your plants, mulch can minimize weeds and cut down on time spent watering. On paths, weed cloth or mulch can help to smother out unwanted sprouts. Make sure to remove your weeds before they go to seed, sending hundreds of their offspring into your garden.

Compost happens whether you manage your pile on a detailed schedule or just dump and run. For the sake of saving time, Whitney switched from a small worm bin to a large dump-and-run compost pile in a semi-shaded area, a placement that also reduced watering. She only turns it once or twice a year and can dig to the bottom of the pile to mine finished compost when needed. Extending a soaker hose or a micro sprinkler from your automated irrigation system can be a good way to maintain a moist pile without much effort. The ideal moisture for a compost pile is about that of a wrung-out sponge—a concept even young kids can grasp and learn to assess. So, if you auto-irrigate your pile, do so on a less-frequent cycle, like one used for perennials or fruit trees, rather than connecting it to the more frequent irrigation system you may have on annuals. Overwatering your pile can make the pile go anaerobic, which can get stinky and slow the composting process.

Another time-saving composting strategy we have seen is building a compost pile in the space of a future garden bed. After the pile is finished composting, some is used to fertilize other beds while the remaining compost is dug in place and turned into a well-amended garden bed.

Remember, gardens aren't instant—they grow over time. From brainstorming fun garden features with your kids to building or revamping your garden together, go easy on yourselves. If you're putting in a new garden from scratch, remember that it's okay to dream big and start small. In fact, this is probably the best approach, so that you and your kids end up with a garden you can manage and enjoy. Day after day, your plants will grow, as will your confidence with gardening. As seasons and years go by, you can bet that your garden will get better and better.

*Ready for the next digging project.*

# Chapter 2

# DIGGING IN WITH KIDS:
# PLAYING, GROWING, THRIVING

---

**SNEAK PEEK: Becoming a mud pie master •
Sowing seeds with small hands • Bean babies •
Creative containers • and more**

*Greta and Neli are off to play while Amy and John finish gathering.*

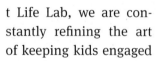

**A**t Life Lab, we are constantly refining the art of keeping kids engaged and interested in gardening. Whether turning a compost pile or starting seeds for spring, here are two rules of thumb we always try to keep in mind.

### RULE #1: INVITE KIDS TO JOIN IN OR NOT, AS THEY CHOOSE

If you go to a friend's house for dinner, and he says that his 7-year-old son, Matthew, and he made a pie together, you know that Matthew probably did just a few things; maybe he cracked an egg or stirred sugar into the crust dough. It definitely took an adult to shepherd the project along, but the goal of involving Matthew presumably went beyond cutting down on the labor involved. The same will be true in gardening with kids.

It is not very likely that your kids will dramatically decrease your garden workload. In fact, you might find that including them requires more work than going it alone. The rewards, however, will make any extra work well worth the effort, as you'll see when you and your kids share the delight of finding the season's first ripe tomato, or are stopped in your tracks by a newly spun spider web catching the morning dew.

If you are an avid, production-oriented home gardener who wants to keep your children occupied so that you can spend as much time as possible working in the garden, remember to be on the lookout for ways your kids can contribute. Most young children, for instance, like to dig. If you show them how to break up dirt clods, they can help you with bed prep. One gardening mother told us that her 4-year-old son could be occupied for long stretches by skimming the paths and returning soil to the garden beds. This was a great task for her child because he could do it without many mistakes, and it left him with a sense of accomplishment. Toward this end, we have suggested age-appropriate tasks for each gardening phase.

If, however, you get the sense that your kids would rather be playing, we suggest that you encourage just that. After all, if your goal is that your kids spend quality time with you, gain a sense of connection to the outdoors, learn to appreciate where food comes from, or just discover a love of gardening, what better way than for them to develop a bank of positive memories out in the garden?

Kris is a gardener, ranger, and mother of two in Alaska. She mentioned that she always did the vast majority of the weeding in her garden, recognizing that it was a turnoff for her kids. She never pushed the issue, and just let them enjoy harvesting and playing while she worked. When she had to leave one summer, however, her kids naturally rose to the occasion and took care of the garden, opening and closing the greenhouses, and watering and weeding every day. Having had years of positive experiences in the garden, Kelly, at age 15, and Stephen, at 12, recognized that the garden harvest they considered central to their summer required a certain amount of work, and so it was worth it to them to take charge.

### RULE #2: REMOVE ROADBLOCKS AND PLAN DIVERSIONS

Whenever you head out to the garden, no one should hesitate to get filthy. So put away those new white pants and take out your oldest pairs

*Laurel's family takes a break from working and playing in the garden for a family snapshot.*

*Trish harvests, Lee jumps—there's more to family gardening than just gardening.*

of jeans. You may also want to set up a station at the door for when you come back in, a place where you and your kids can leave muddy boots and change into slippers. Once outside, you don't want there to be any excuse for you or your kids to stay clean.

Diversions can be useful, too. A child may talk about harvesting peas all day, but then get out to the garden and tire of harvesting in just a few minutes. Therefore, we have included ideas for playful activities related to each of your own tasks. Your kids may make mud pies while you prepare the soil for planting, for example. Or maybe you'll decide to make mud pies together and save the soil preparation for another time. Many parents just like to have their kids out with them, no matter how their activities relate to the gardening task at hand.

Kyle's family garden blooms year-round.

Lee (age 10), for example, often suggests to his mom that they go out in the garden, where he jumps on the trampoline while Trish does whatever needs doing. Has he developed a sense of connection to the garden? Absolutely. He loves giving people tours, and whenever friends come over, they spend the majority of their time outside. Trish has given Lee his own bed to plant, and he brims with excitement when sharing what he has planted and what his plans are for the bed. His enthusiasm for the garden comes from spending loads of time out there with his mom, and being invited, but not pressured, to get involved in gardening tasks along the way.

## Planning What to Plant

There is enormous variation in the degree to which families plan their gardens. Some simply look outside one spring day and say, "Okay, the soil is ready to work. Let's go to the nursery and see what looks good." Others spend countless winter hours snuggled together by the fireplace, poring over seed catalogs and dreaming of the growing season ahead. Some make detailed spreadsheets together, counting days before their average last frost date to determine when they can safely start their seeds. Still others employ online resources to help their gardens take shape. All of these families achieve a harvest. By carefully selecting which plants to grow and when, however, the planning family is able to maximize their harvest of the garden plants they treasure most.

Crop planning also provides a delightful way to keep up your family's connection to the garden between growing seasons. As you walk through nurseries and thumb through seed catalogs with your kids, they will start to build anticipation for the growing season ahead. When you go to the nursery, you might even give your kids a little money to choose seeds or plants they want to grow themselves. One mother told us that when her kids were young, sometimes the Easter Bunny brought them seeds instead of candy.

There is no greater way to teach your kids about deferred gratification than by involving them in planning and ordering seeds in the winter, starting the seeds indoors in the late winter or early spring, transplanting them into the garden in spring, watching them grow throughout the spring and summer, and finally harvesting the fruits of their labor all summer and fall. When we asked one 3-year-old Life Lab camper about her favorite things to do in the garden, her eyes lit up as she said, "Eating something after waiting a long, long time."

We have found that tracking our gardens through the seasons is a great way to teach our own children about natural cycles. John makes a point of showing Neli how things decompose in the garden at the end of the growing season, and boasts to adult friends by having Neli define "deciduous." Novice gardeners often have a hard time understanding what grows when, but you can use your garden as a tool to impart this knowledge to your children. In general, root, stem, leaf, and flower bud plants are cool season crops while fruits and seeds are warm season crops. This is a concept that children can grasp.

The difference between perennials and annuals is another concept that your children will begin to comprehend after a couple seasons of replanting annuals and observing perennial shrubs and trees in the same spot year after year.

By planting perennials in your garden, your plans will bear fruit for years to come. If you live in an area with mild winters, you can plant fruit trees for a year-round harvest. Trish and her family eat their way from apples to pears in the fall, persimmons to oranges and lemons in the winter, and plums to nectarines in the summer. You can do something similar with flowers, so that your perennial flower garden looks vibrant year-round. Winter and early spring can bring daffodils, forsythia and tulips. Summer bursts with blooms such as dahlias, delphiniums, and rudbeckia. The end of the year closes with asters, mums, and sneezeweed, to name a few.

Crop planning involves a delicate balance between colorful daydreaming and cold, hard math. Some kids may be more interested in selecting the prettiest orange flower for the front stoop, while others will focus on counting down days until the average last frost date has passed. We will outline activities that run the gamut, to help any child engage in crop planning.

# Smart PLANNING for Small SPACES

*Sharon's small yard in a suburban neighborhood turns out a bounty of edibles.*

SHARON'S 7- AND 10-YEAR-OLD daughters are master foragers, but they did not become this way by accident. Sharon has filled her 50 × 100-foot suburban yard with 15 fruit trees, 10 types of berries, and a rambling passion fruit vine. Her daughters have tuned into the seasons and await the coming sweet treats that their garden provides. When they are not snacking on fruit and berries, they are picking edible flowers such as borage, nasturtium, chrysanthemum, and miniature blossoms of rosemary and thyme. Sharon calls it a nibbling garden and knows that she can always send her kids to the garden to search for edible treats.

So how does Sharon pack all that in a small space, along with the annual veggies and herbs that they grow? Through careful planning. She has selected tree varieties on dwarfing rootstocks and some trees are planted two or three to a hole. In some instances, multiple varieties of fruit are grafted on a single tree. Maintaining a garden like this takes a different type of care. For example, summer pruning is often needed to keep closely spaced trees from overtaking their neighbor's yard. For more information on prolonged harvest of tree-ripened fruit in small spaces, check out Colby Eierman's book, *Fruit Trees in Small Spaces: Abundant Harvests from Your Own Backyard,* or visit davewilson.com/homegrown/gardencompass/gc01_mar_apr_01.html.

# Turn into a Tourist

Take your kids on a tour of a local garden or farm to get ideas of what you might grow in your own garden. Even experienced gardeners can get new ideas from other people's garden plots. You and your family can also visit botanical gardens, farm stands, and farmers' markets in search of exciting plants to grow in your garden. Just remember that the produce at the farm stands and markets will be in its harvest season, so you may have to wait awhile until it is time to plant those crops again.

**HERE'S WHAT YOU'LL NEED:**

1 notebook and pen or pencil

Access to a local garden or farm

1 camera

Seed catalogs or planting guides

*You can find community gardens near you at communitygarden.org/. To order information for seed catalogs, see organicgardening. com/learn-and-grow/seed-catalog-time.*

**HERE'S WHAT YOU'LL DO:**

1 Visit a local garden or farm. Take a walk around and note the plants they have growing. If there are any plants you don't recognize, see if there is a gardener there you can ask.

2 Note which plants you might like to grow in your garden. Take pictures of each one.

3 When you return home, make a book of pictures from your tour. Look up each one in your seed catalog or planting guide. Next to each plant, write down the plant name and important information, such as when to plant, days to harvest, and growing requirements.

4 Use this book as you create a planting calendar for the following growing season.

# ENJOYING BOTANICAL ADVENTURES AS A FAMILY

SALLIE'S FAMILY HAS had their fair share of botanical adventures. Sallie says her husband, Ben, knows of every rose and dahlia garden in Oregon, and their family has visited many botanical gardens, from the Living Desert in Palm Desert, California, to Butchart Gardens in Victoria, British Columbia. Having a plant geek dad has its benefits for 9-year-old twin boys Miles and Blake–they vividly recall their visit to the California Carnivores in Sebastopol, California. The boys also get paid to tend to their father's roses, and every year they get to pick out a new type of plant to try out in their garden. Squirting cucumbers, hairy summer squash, giant pumpkins, cacti, carnivorous plants, and even mushrooms have all seen time in their garden. Sallie has completed the Master Gardener program and gives back by caring for the worms at her son's school garden. Whether at home or on vacation, Sallie, Ben, Miles, and Blake can be found having botanical adventures. Sallie says the garden makes her family feel good and brings the web of life in front of their eyes.

For lists of gardens to visit in the United States, Canada, and the United Kingdom, search gardenvisit.com and rhs.org.uk/Shows-Events/Regional-events. In the United States, publicgardens.org/gardens is also a great resource.

Ben and Sallie's favorite garden catalogs include Baker Seed Company, The Cook's Garden, David Austin Roses, Heirloom Roses, High Country Gardens, Renee's Garden Seeds, Seed Savers Exchange, Territorial Seed Company, Vintage Gardens, Wayside Gardens, and White Flower Farm.

# Creating a Plant Collage

This is a great activity for those fall and winter months. Brew some tea, get a fire going, and make a night of browsing garden and seed catalogs together with your children. You can make a collage of plants you like or plants you would like to grow in your garden. Don't worry too much about actual planning with these collages. The idea here is simply to engage your kids in looking through the catalog and thinking about the planting possibilities.

## HERE'S WHAT YOU'LL NEED:

- Seed and garden catalogs
- Scissors
- Cardstock
- Glue

*For ordering information for seed catalogs, see organicgardening.com/learn-and-grow/ seed-catalog-time.*

## HERE'S WHAT YOU'LL DO:

1. Look through a seed catalog together. Go on a mini treasure hunt through the catalog, looking for the most beautiful flower, the best-looking tomato, the longest carrot, the brightest yellow, or anything else that strikes your fancy.

2. Cut out pictures of plants that delight you. If your kids are young, have them choose any plant. If they are older, have them check the growing region and limit their selections to things that grow in your area.

3. Arrange the pictures of plants in any design you like. Glue the pictures onto the cardstock to make a garden collage.

4. Hang your garden collage in your house. Look to it when you need some inspiration for what to plant next in your garden.

## ALSO TRY THIS:

Draw a basic map of your garden and then you and your kids can glue pictures of plants into the beds, making your collage look like your real garden in full bloom.

# Making Planting Calendars

Dreaming of next year's garden at Sallie's home.

Thumb through seed catalogs or planting guides with your kids, choose plants that you like and that grow well in your area, and make a calendar for when to plant each one. For older kids, this is a great chance to practice math.

## HERE'S WHAT YOU'LL NEED:

Paper and pencil

Calendar

Seed catalogs

## HERE'S WHAT YOU'LL DO:

1. Find your region's average last spring frost date and mark it on your calendar. You can search online at victoryseeds.com/info.html to find frost dates for Canada and the United States. For suggested frost dates in the United Kingdom visit gardenaction.co.uk/main/weather1.asp. Remember, the last frost may fall a few weeks before or after this average date, so prepare to protect your seeds, or mark 2 weeks after your average last frost date as your safe last frost date.

2. Look at your seed catalog and list all of the crops you want to grow. For each one, read the description to find out if it should be started indoors or sown directly into the garden. Also read about its cold tolerance to determine when to plant it in relation to your average last frost date. Mark planting dates on your calendar. For example, your conversation might go something like this: "We can plant tomato seedlings outdoors 2 weeks after our average last frost date. If our average last frost date is March 31, when can we plant the tomatoes?" (Count forward 2 weeks on the calendar and mark the date). "Okay, if we want to plant tomato seedlings on April 14 and they take about 6 weeks to grow indoors, when should we start the seeds?" (Count backwards 6 weeks from April 14). Useful seed starting date calculators can be found at johnnyseeds.com.

3. Continue with this process until you have dates set for all the seeds you hope to start and all the seedlings you hope to transplant into the garden. If you want certain crops available for as much of the year as possible, you will want to plan multiple, or successive, sowings.

## ALSO TRY THIS:

If you want to plan a harvest for a specific time, show your children how to use the days until harvest information in the seed catalog to determine when to plant each crop. This is helpful if you are growing food for a specific holiday or event. It can also help you determine how to stagger your planting if you want to harvest multiple crops together for one big feast.

## Preparing Garden Beds

"Don't track dirt into the house!" "Don't use dirty words!" "Stop right there—your hands are dirty!" Kids hear a lot about dirt every day, but how often do they hear us singing dirt's praises? Of course, germs are real and hand washing is important. But as gardeners, we are always eager to balance the cautionary news on dirt with the good. Dirt is just soil where it is not supposed to be. When children pick and eat fresh food right from a plant, they see firsthand how soil could be considered more precious than gold. Without soil, they begin to realize, we would not have anything to eat. It can be fun to challenge your kids to come up with something that they eat (or wear for that matter) that does not require soil to grow. For anything they mention, see if you can trace it back to a plant or animal source and, ultimately, back to the soil.

Gardeners work most directly with the soil when they are first preparing a bed for planting, so this is a great time to engage kids in the business of getting dirty. Your kids may rather just play with dirt while you prepare the bed; that's great. Many parents would consider that a first step on the path to growing a lifelong gardener.

Your children may also want to get involved in preparing the bed with you. In that case, here are some kid-friendly tasks for them.

### Clear the Bed

While you are pulling out spent plants, invite your kids to join you, and ask for their help in pulling

*Caitlin's boys have claimed a pile of dirt as their own, but that's fine with her.*

*Mud body paint makes its mark.*

out the toughest plants. If you are not pulling everything out of the bed, make sure to show your kids which plants to leave. Have them show you which plants they're leaving alone, to make double sure they understand. You can also make sure keeper plants aren't pulled out accidentally by marking them with plant labels or small branches.

While many adults find weeding relaxing, most kids only like it for about 5 minutes or so. Follow their lead and have alternate activities ready, such as a pit where they can dig, or crayons and paper for drawing in the garden. There will be plenty of gardening tasks for them to get involved in later.

## Add Compost

Once your bed is weeded, kids of all ages can help you sift the compost. They can use a small-holed nursery tray or a compost sifter, made with a piece of metal hardware cloth stretched between two pieces of wood. Alternately, they can just put on garden gloves and use their hands. Kids love to spread shovelfuls of finished compost onto a tarp and then return worms and other decomposers back to the compost pile, along with items that need more time to fully decompose. Then they can bring buckets or wheelbarrows full of finished, sifted compost to the garden beds and, using tools their size, spread a layer of compost over the bed.

## Dig and Shape the Bed

Once you're ready to turn the compost in, older kids can use digging forks or spades and work right alongside you. If you have a few younger helpers, put away the digging forks and work together with hand trowels to blend in the compost and break up the soil. If this is a new bed, with compacted earth, some work with large tools may be required to break up the soil to a depth of about 1 foot. If you're simply turning over an already-dug bed, hand trowels should suffice. Finally, have your kids use a rake, hand tools, or just their hands to smooth out the entire bed. Most kids love to collect dirt clods and break them up, so invite them to do this after each pass with the rake.

Be aware that children tend to pat down newly prepped soil, often to the point of over-compaction. If you find your kids compacting the soil, remind them that the bed needs to be loose and fluffy for water, air, and roots to travel downward. At Life Lab, we illustrate this point by having kids imagine that they are plants and

CONTINUED ON PAGE 72

PROJECT

# Creative Containers

You and your kids can create planting containers from ordinary household items. There are many options: empty yogurt cups, empty recipe boxes, small milk cartons, wooden boxes, barrels, old wagons, old boots, and old wheelbarrows, just to name a few.

**HERE'S WHAT YOU'LL NEED:**

Containers that are at least 2 inches deep, with drainage holes added if none exist

Drill or nail for making drainage holes

Seed-starting mix

Seeds

Access to water

**HERE'S WHAT YOU'LL DO:**

1. Gather containers. You might look in your own recycling bin, or head to a local thrift store and check out the knickknacks. Make sure your containers are at least 2 inches deep. Clean each container well.

2. Drill or puncture drainage holes in the bottom of each container. If you want to, you can also decorate your containers.

3. Fill the containers with seed-starting mix.

4. Plant seeds in the containers. Water and watch them grow.

**ALSO TRY THIS:**

If you're planting wheat, chives, or anything that might look like hair, draw faces on the sides of your container, leaving the tops of the heads open to let your plant grow up and make funny hairdos.

# Becoming a Mud Pie Master

*Voilà! A masterpiece.*

Take advantage of a sunny day to stir up some garden soil and water to make memorable mud pies with your kids.

## HERE'S WHAT YOU'LL DO:

1. Fill a pie tin with soil. Use your hands to break up the clods.

2. Pour water over the soil, a little at a time. Stir with the stick until you have thick, pasty mud.

3. Take a walk around the garden or neighborhood and collect flowers, leaves, bark, fruits, twigs, and any other objects that you think would look nice on your pie.

4. Decorate the top of your pie and set it in a sunny place to dry.

5. Check your pie every few hours. Once dry, use your mud pie as a centerpiece on your table or feed it to your hungry compost pile.

## ALSO TRY THIS:

*Soil soup, anyone?*

In a variation on this activity, you can make a soil soup. Simply pour soil into a bucket and add water. Let your budding chef determine the best consistency. Stir in rocks, sticks, leaves, and other objects from the garden. Pour into smaller bowls or into holes in the ground. If your soup dries out before your child's interest does, stir in more water to make it soupy again.

## HERE'S WHAT YOU'LL NEED:

1 pie tin

1 hand trowel

1 full watering can

1 stirring stick

Access to soil that can be dug up

# *Discovering Soil Horizons*

H elp your kids learn about the soil texture in your garden by creating a layered soil sample, or a soil horizon, in a jar. You never know—you may learn something, too.

**HERE'S WHAT YOU'LL NEED:**

1 clear, plastic or glass quart-sized jar with lid

1 hand trowel

Access to soil that can be dug up

Water

Soil type chart

**HERE'S WHAT YOU'LL DO:**

1 Fill your jar about two-thirds full with water.

2 Take a soil sample. To do this, use your trowel to remove the top inch or so of soil from a small area. Then dig out soil from underneath and fill about half the jar with soil, then top off the jar with water.

3 Seal the jar completely and shake it vigorously.

4 Place the jar somewhere and leave it, undisturbed, for at least 24 hours, checking it every once in awhile to observe changes.

5 When you return to your jar, you should see different layers of soil at the bottom of the jar. Gravity causes the different-sized soil particles to separate. The bottom layer is sand, next up is silt, and the top layer is clay.

6 Use the soil type chart to determine what kind of soil you have in your garden. For kids old enough to grasp fractions and percentages, this is a great opportunity to practice some basic math. For younger kids, look together at the soil type chart and ask which looks most like the sample you have in your jar.

CONTINUED →

6 Compare soil in different parts of your garden, or in different gardens. Different types of soil retain water differently. Specifically, clay-rich soils retain moisture and nutrients for longer periods of time than sandy soils, and sandy soils drain more rapidly than clay-rich soils. You can use this information when trying to determine how frequently to water your garden. For instance, about an hour after you and your kids have watered a bed, return to it to check the moisture in the soil. Do the same after 12 and 24 hours, each time talking about where the water went and when you think it will be time to water again.

# USE THIS CHART & YOUR SOIL SHAKE JAR

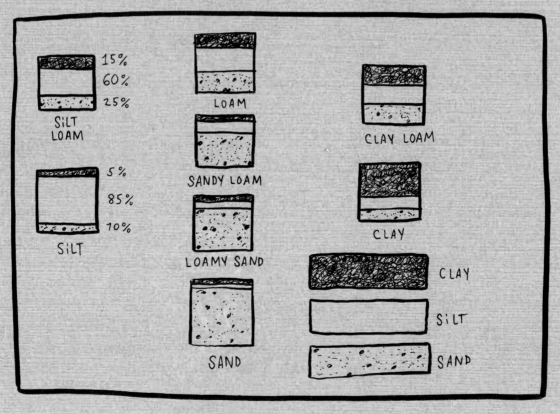

# Becoming a Soil Scientist—
# Testing Your Soil

Choose organic amendments for your family's garden.

**E**ncourage young chemists by using a soil test kit to determine what nutrients your soil has and what it needs to grow healthy plants.

## HERE'S WHAT YOU'LL NEED:

Soil test kit (available at most garden centers)

Access to soil that can be dug up

1 hand trowel

## HERE'S WHAT YOU'LL DO:

1. Gather a trowel full of garden soil, following any specific directions given in your soil test kit.

2. Follow the directions in your soil test kit to find out how much nitrogen, phosphorous, and potassium your garden soil has.

3. Use your results to determine what your soil has and what it needs. If you need nitrogen, you can add blood meal or composted poultry manure. For extra phosphorous, you can add bone meal, fish meal, or rock phosphate. Potassium can be added with composted manure, wood ash, or seaweed. Your local nursery should have these amendments; follow the directions on the product package.

4. Engage your children in the work of young scientists by testing your soil prior to adding amendments and noting what you added. The nutrients in soil amendments, especially organic ones such as those mentioned here, may take months or even years to be fully released into the soil, so re-test every fall and spring to measure their effects.

## ALSO TRY THIS:

Soil test kits are a great tool for kids' garden experiments. Test your soil before and after planting cover crops or adding compost, to measure changes.

→ CONTINUED FROM PAGE 67

using their fingers to dig roots into the soil. We have them contrast what it would feel like to grow roots in the bed as compared with the path.

After your bed is prepared, you or an older child can test it by dropping in a digging fork, spade, or hand trowel, point down. If it penetrates and stands on its own, you know you have a well-dug bed. When finished, make sure to take a moment to step back together and appreciate how you have transformed the garden bed.

## Planting the Seeds of Future Harvests

What could be more awe-inspiring to a child (or an adult for that matter) than watching a hard seed, no larger than a pebble, burst with life? Seeds come in all shapes, colors, and sizes. Some are uniquely designed to take flight in the slightest breeze, while others stick to your socks like Velcro (in fact, plant seeds clinging to the inventor's clothes were the inspiration for Velcro). Some are edible, others poisonous. Because seeds are so diverse and so fascinating for children and adults alike, we have suggested not only ways to plant them with kids, but also ways to explore them further as a family—by saving and collecting them, dissecting them, and even using them to create art.

As any parent who has attempted it will tell you, there is an art to planting seeds with kids. Small seeds especially present challenges for small hands. Life Lab has developed several tried-and-true tips for sowing seeds successfully with children.

*Trish and Lee get a jump on the season by starting seeds in their greenhouse. • It takes concentration to not miss a seed.*

## Starting Seeds Indoors

Experienced gardeners are well aware of the benefits of starting some seeds indoors. While certain seeds, such as carrots, beets, and peas, thrive sown directly into garden beds outdoors, others, such as tomatoes and eggplant, grow better when started in small containers indoors. Starting seeds indoors also provides enthusiastic gardeners with the opportunity to extend their growing season and hit the ground running with homegrown seedlings when the soil is ready for planting.

When kids are involved, starting seeds indoors provides yet another benefit: it is gardening on a child's scale. Just as kids enjoy tiny action figures or dolls, so, too, do they delight in watching baby plants grow in small containers in their home. Many children take great care in watering seeds and are jubilant when their baby plants emerge.

Kids of all ages can help find objects to reuse for planting containers. Older kids can help drill

## USING Farmer MEASUREMENTS FOR Planting

TALK TO ANY farmer or avid gardener, and it is likely that she will know the approximate width of her fist, and the distance from the tip of her thumb to pinkie on her outstretched hand. This is because farmers and gardeners have to estimate measurements all the time, and they do not like to run inside for rulers.

Help your kids find their own farmer measurements on their bodies. Simply take out a ruler and have them measure the width of their fist with fingers tightly

*Knowing farmer measurements is very handy in the garden for spacing seeds and transplants.*

clenched, then the distance from their thumbtip to pinky with their fingers outstretched. Next, have them find their personal inch, measuring from each fingertip to each knuckle until they get one that is close to an inch. Once kids

know a few approximate measurements on their bodies, they can call upon this knowledge when spacing seeds or seedlings. We often explain to kids, "These seeds need to be planted half an inch deep. That means you will push them in as deep as the first knuckle on your index finger." Or, "Plant these seedlings every 12 inches. You can measure three fist-lengths between each seedling." Of course, your kids are growing, so their measurements will change over time.

or poke drainage holes in the bottoms of the containers. Then everyone can fill the containers with seed-starting mix. We always do this outdoors or over a large bucket, because some seed-starting mix is bound to land outside of the containers. Then we read the seed packets or planting guides together with the kids to determine how deep to plant the seeds. When we're ready to plant, we teach kids of all ages to use their farmer measurements to drill seeds into the seed-starting mix with their fingers.

Seed spacing also provides parents with plentiful opportunities to reinforce math skills at home. Teachers in Life Lab's school garden workshops engage kids in fun, hands-on measurement activities while also teaching them about seed spacing. For example, you can make sowing strings by marking a string at regular intervals, such as every 3 inches. Tie a stick to each end of your string and push the sticks into each end of the bed. Use this as a guide to help you plant every 3, 6, 9, or 12 inches. You can also make your own, plantable seed tape.

Once your kids have sown their seeds and covered them with seed-starting mix, have them water gently every day, making sure the soil never dries out. Since most seeds prefer soil that is kept consistently moist, and most kids will want to check on their seeds at least daily, make a ritual of it. Every day at breakfast, lunch, and dinner, for example, have your kids check to make sure the soil is moist, and water if it seems to be drying out. A spray bottle or kid-sized watering can with a sprinkling spout is very helpful at this stage to prevent inadvertent overwatering, which can drown a seed.

## Sowing Seeds Directly Outdoors

Some seeds thrive when sown directly into garden beds. There are three methods of direct sowing: broadcasting, furrow planting, and drilling. After years of practice, we have found tricks to make each method work with young children.

### BROADCASTING

The broadcasting approach is best for tiny seeds such as cut-and-come lettuce or wildflowers. It entails sprinkling seeds relatively evenly over the soil and then covering them with a thin layer of soil. This can be difficult for tiny hands, and often kids will end up pouring a pile of tiny seeds in one place. To make broadcasting easier, we recommend mixing your seeds with sand. This way, kids can sprinkle big handfuls of seeds and sand over the soil and only scatter a small number of seeds. Because the sand is a different color than the soil, this also allows you to see where seeds have and have not been scattered. If you choose to use beach sand, be sure to rinse it well to remove any salt. You can purchase nursery grade sand that has been rinsed and is often more coarse than beach or river sand.

### FURROW PLANTING

The second method of sowing seeds directly involves digging a small trench as deep as you want to plant, then scattering the seeds evenly down the trench and filling it in with soil. This method works well for medium-sized seeds, such as beets, and also for plants you intend to thin after they emerge, such as carrots. In the case of a plant you will be sowing densely and thinning later, adding rinsed sand can again be helpful.

*A spray bottle makes watering newly planted seeds manageable and fun.*

If you want to space your seeds evenly, you can have your kids dig the trench. Then have them work with you to place each seed. With younger kids, it may work best if you put a seed down, then have them use their farmer measurements to measure ahead and tell you where to place the next seed, until the entire row is full. Once all of your seeds are spaced down the trench, your kids can fill it in with soil.

### DRILLING

Because big seeds are involved, most parents consider drilling the most kid-friendly seed-sowing method. Kids can use their farmer measurements to map out where each seed will go. Have them mark each spot by placing the seed on top of the soil. Once all seeds are placed, stand back and make sure they look well distributed, and then have your kids use a finger to drill in the seeds to the appropriate depth, again using farmer measurements. Have them cover the seeds with soil.

### WATERING IN

Once your seeds are planted, it is important to water them in. Be sure to supervise if your kids are doing the watering—newly planted seeds are vulnerable, and it's easy for a child to deliver too much or not enough water. Creative ideas like using a spray bottle help protect your plantings.

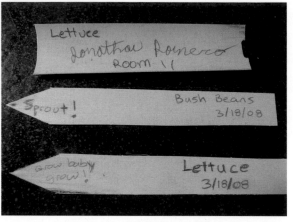

*Discarded plastic blinds make great plant labels.*

## MAKING PLANT LABELS

How often have you planted seeds and thought, "I'll remember what I planted here," only to forget? Plant labels help parents and kids alike remember what they have planted where, and also provide a space for recording important information, such as planting dates, days to germination, watering requirements, and the like. For kids, plant labels also provide an opportunity to practice writing and to develop a sense of connection and ownership to the plants-to-be before they emerge. In addition to important planting information, it can be fun to have your kids write a wish for a plant on the label and then stick it in the soil.

PROJECT

# On the Hunt for Seeds, Seeds, Seeds

On a fall day, take your kids on a treasure hunt for seeds of all kinds.

### HERE'S WHAT YOU'LL NEED:

A small container or paper bag to hold each collector's seeds

### HERE'S WHAT YOU'LL DO:

1 Head outdoors into a garden or forest, or just take a walk through your neighborhood.

2 Look for seeds everywhere you go. Check inside flowers, pods, cones, and fruits, as well as on the ground underneath trees and shrubs.

3 Shake plants to see what seeds fall out.

4 Your kids might like to do any number of things with the seeds they find. Follow their lead. They may want to count them, draw them, collect and plant them, or make a map showing where each was found.

### ALSO TRY THIS:

Head into your kitchen for another treasure hunt, this time for edible seeds. Remember, in addition to the seeds inside of fruits and some vegetables, nuts, peas, and beans are seeds. Grains are also seeds, often ground into flour. So consider bread, rice, pasta, and other wheat or grain products in your hunt. Your kids may be surprised to discover how many seeds are around us every day.

# Seedy Mosaics

*A seedy new art form.*

**U**se a variety of seeds to make colorful mosaic artwork with your kids.

## HERE'S WHAT YOU'LL NEED:

Cardboard square

Glue

A variety of seeds

*You can collect seeds from plants and trees in your garden and neighborhood; from old, expired seed packets; or from a grocery store. The bulk bins in many natural food stores tend to have beans, nuts, and other seeds of various shapes, sizes, and colors. Many dried soup mixes also contain a diverse selection of seeds.*

## HERE'S WHAT YOU'LL DO:

1. Create a design on your cardboard with glue. You might draw an animal, a spiral, or a landscape, for example.

2. Sprinkle seeds over all of the glue on your paper. If you want particular seeds in particular places, you may choose to place them by hand.

3. Allow the glue to dry. Shake the loose seeds off the paper.

4. Hang your seed mosaic on the wall and enjoy some natural beauty indoors.

## ALSO TRY THIS:

Make a seed mosaic picture of your garden and incorporate some leftover seeds from the plants you have been growing. For example, include sunflower seeds when adding sunflowers to your picture.

*Nadine and Neli work on a seed mosaic at a garden-themed party.*

# Seedy Socks

**Take a walk on the wild side and see what sticks.**

Late in the season, once many plants have gone to seed, take a walk through a meadow and see what seeds stick to your socks. Your kids might be interested to know that this is the way Velcro was invented. A Swiss engineer, Georges de Mestral, was on a hunting trip with his dog. The burrs (seeds) of burdock that stuck to his pants and his dog's fur inspired him to create a fastening system based on nature's design of the hook-topped seeds.

Once you've gleaned the seeds from your socks, plant them together and watch what emerges.

*This activity only works late in the growing season, once plants have gone to seed. Depending on your location, this can range from late summer to autumn.*

## HERE'S WHAT YOU'LL NEED:

1 old, oversized sock

1 planting container

Seed-starting mix

Water

## HERE'S WHAT YOU'LL DO:

1 Place the old sock over your shoe.

2 Take a walk through a meadow, dragging your sock right through the grasses and plants.

3 Take a look at your sock. When it has some seeds stuck to it, take it off and bring it home.

4 Look closely at the seeds and see if you can figure out how they stuck to your socks. Some might have corkscrew-like extensions that screw into fabric; others might have hooks or a sticky substance.

5 At home, plant your entire sock in a container with seed-starting mix. Keep it watered and watch what grows.

## PROJECT

# Bean Babies

**W**ear a seed around your neck and watch it germinate.

### HERE'S WHAT YOU'LL NEED:

*The necklace that grows on you.*

1 small plastic jewelry bag (about 2 × 3 inches) with a zip-lock top

String

Scissors or a hole punch

1 cotton ball

Access to water

1 large seed, such as a fava or scarlet runner bean

### HERE'S WHAT YOU'LL DO:

1. Wet the cotton ball and wring it out. Place the damp cotton ball and seed inside the plastic bag and seal the bag.

2. Punch a hole in the top of the bag. Cut a piece of string long enough to make a necklace that you can place over your head. Thread the string through the hole to make a necklace.

3. Help your kids hang the bags around their necks. Their body heat will keep the seeds warm. Seed necklaces should be worn all day long, with the bag opened occasionally to allow for air flow. Place necklaces somewhere warm at night.

4. Wear the seed day after day, and watch as a plant begins to emerge.

## PROJECT

# Seeds from the Inside Out

*Soaking a seed overnight loosens its exterior, so you can see what's inside.*

**H**elp your kids split seeds in half and discover the baby plant inside.

### HERE'S WHAT YOU'LL NEED:

1 large bean, such as a fava, lima, pinto, or scarlet runner bean

Magnifying glass

### HERE'S WHAT YOU'LL DO:

1. Soak your bean in water for at least 8 hours or overnight.

2. Split your soaked seed in half. To do this, slide your fingernail along the thin edge of the curved side of the seed, allowing it to split naturally. Gently pry apart the 2 halves.

3. Use your magnifying glass to look at the inside of the seed. See if you can find the root, the shoot, and the baby leaves. See if you can find veins inside the baby leaves.

# Let's See What's Sproutin'

*Our indoor sproutin' tray is tended by Neli.*

G row and enjoy your own edible sprout snacks with your kids.

**HERE'S WHAT YOU'LL NEED:**

1 quart-sized glass jar

1 (4-inch) square cheesecloth to cover the jar

1 rubber band

1 teaspoon

$1/4$ pound alfalfa seeds (available in bulk bins at grocery stores)

1 roll paper towels

**HERE'S WHAT YOU'LL DO:**

1. Pour 2 teaspoonfuls of alfalfa seeds into the jar, and add water to just cover the seeds.

2. Cover the jar with the cheesecloth and secure it with the rubber band. Set the seeds in a closet, cupboard, or other dark place.

3. The next day, turn the jar upside down to drain the water into the sink. Pour clean water over the seeds and drain again. Then set the jar in a sunny place, such as a windowsill.

4. Soak and drain the seeds twice a day for 4 days.

5. Around the 4th day, when the little seedlings are 2 to 3 inches long and bright green, they are ready to eat.

6. Eat your sprouts plain, add them to a salad, or coat an apple with nut butter and roll in the sprouts for a fuzzy snack.

# *Saving Seeds for Next Season*

*Hollyhock seeds make for easy seed saving.*

HOLLYHOCK

**H**elp your kids gather seeds from your garden and store them to plant in the next growing season.

## HERE'S WHAT YOU'LL NEED:

- Small manila coin envelopes (one for each packet of seeds you wish to make)
- Colored pencils or pens
- Newspaper
- A small paper bag
- Plants with fully grown seeds: Good candidates include sunflowers, beans, peas, lettuce, cilantro, fennel, dill, amaranth, spinach, basil, hollyhock, calendula, peppers, and poppies

## HERE'S WHAT YOU'LL DO:

1. On a sunny day, take a walk around your garden and look for plants with fully grown seeds.

2. Gather seeds from each plant. For sunflowers, collect the entire flower heads; for beans and peas, collect the pods; for corn, collect ears; for lettuce, place a paper bag under the flowering stalk and shake it to let the seeds fall into the bag; and for cilantro, fennel, dill, angelica, and amaranth, remove whole, dried out flowers.

3. Place everything on newspaper in a dry, sunny place and allow the seeds to dry out for about a week.

4. Decorate envelopes for each type of seed you collected. You may choose to include a picture of the fully grown plant, planting information, or pictures of the seeds. Be sure to include the date on which you collected the seeds.

5. Remove the dried seeds from their pods, flowers, or ears and store in the envelopes in a cool, dry space.

6. Plant your seeds the following year, or give them to other gardeners as gifts.

# Planet-Friendly Paper Pots

These transplants are ready to plant with or without their paper pots.

**M**ake paper pots with your kids to learn about reusing a common piece of household trash. You can purchase a wooden pot maker at kidsgardening.org or use a full, unopened 5.5-ounce juice can.

## HERE'S WHAT YOU'LL NEED:

- Scissors
- Old newspaper
- A pot maker
- Seed-starting mix
- Seeds
- An empty nursery tray or milk carton cut in half lengthwise

*Getting ready to roll up the pot.*

*All rolled up.*

*Tucking in the bottom of pot.*

*Sealing the bottom.*

## HERE'S WHAT YOU'LL DO:

1. Cut the newspaper into strips 3 × 10 inches wide.

2. Place a newspaper strip on a flat surface, with the short end close to you.

3. Place the pot maker on this same end of the newspaper strip, leaving about 1 1/2 inches of newspaper hanging over the bottom.

4. Roll the pot maker over the table, away from you, to wrap it in newspaper.

5. Fold in the part hanging over the bottom.

6. Turn the pot maker upright and press down on the table.

7. Gently remove the pot maker. You should have a newspaper pot.

8. Make pots for all the seeds you want to plant, and enough to fill a nursery tray or half milk carton.

9. Fill your new pots with seed-starting mix, then place your pots in a nursery tray or milk carton side by side so they are held upright.

10. Plant and label your seeds. Keep them watered and watch them grow.

**Note:** When your seedlings are ready to transplant, you can remove them from the newspaper pots by peeling the newspaper away. You can also plant each seedling in its pot and let the newspaper decompose in the ground. In this case, make sure to bury all of the newspaper completely, so that it does not wick water away from your plant's roots.

*A cut milk carton with holes poked in the bottom holds a pack of seedlings.*

# A Root with a View

**M**ake a root-view cup with your kids and watch your plant's roots grow over time. Some fun plants to watch grow in root-view cups include peas, corn, rainbow chard, big beans such as favas, and nigella flowers, which have colored roots.

*Plant seeds right against the side of the cup.*

## HERE'S WHAT YOU'LL NEED:

- 2 identical soft, clear plastic cups
- Scissors
- 1 nail or drill
- 1 piece of black construction paper
- Pencil or pen
- Tape
- Seed-starting mix
- 1 to 4 seeds
- Access to water

## HERE'S WHAT YOU'LL DO:

1. Take 1 cup and cut a slit from the lip of the cup to the base. Then cut around the base until it falls out. This should leave you with an arc, which you will use as a template to create a cover for your other cup.

2. Lay the arc on a piece of black construction paper and trace it. Add 2 inches to the end and cut out the arc shape from the paper.

3. Drill or poke a few drainage holes in the bottom of your second cup.

4. Fill this cup with seed-starting mix and then plant seeds pressed right along the edges of the cup. You should be able to see your seeds through the sides of the cup.

5. Wrap the black paper arc around this cup until the ends overlap. Tape the ends together, making a sleeve to block the light.

6. Water your seeds and watch them grow. As they grow, you can remove your sleeve occasionally to see the roots grow, too.

## ALSO TRY THIS:

Plant various seeds around the edges of your cup and compare the root systems.

*Root-view cups bring the wonder of the garden indoors. • Dark paper will be wrapped around the cup to keep the light away from the roots.*

*Rat and frog explore the miniature jungle of lettuce.*

┌╴PROJECT╶┐

# Planting a Prehistoric Jungle

P lant a bed of lettuce seeds with your kids. Place some toy dinosaurs or the like in the bed and watch your jungle come to life.

## HERE'S WHAT YOU'LL NEED:

- A garden bed of any size
- Lettuce seeds
- Access to water
- Small toy dinosaurs or other animals

## HERE'S WHAT YOU'LL DO:

1. Prepare your garden bed for planting.
2. Broadcast mixed lettuce seeds over the bed. If you like, you can also include other greens, such as arugula or spinach, and some edible flowers, such as bachelor buttons. For young kids, you can mix the seeds with sand to make broadcasting easier.
3. Place some toy dinosaurs in the bed. As your garden bed grows, it will become a dense prehistoric jungle.

## ALSO TRY THIS:

Make an asparagus forest with miniature hikers, a chard and kale sea floor with miniature fish, or any other miniature landscape you can imagine.

# Homemade Seed Tape

S eed tape makes it much easier for tiny hands to space tiny seeds, such as those of carrots. Making one is as simple as helping your kids paste seeds onto a strip of paper and letting it dry. Then plant the tape, water it in, and watch your garden row grow.

## HERE'S WHAT YOU'LL NEED:

Paper without color printing on it, such as black and white newspaper, paper towels, or a thin paper bag

Scissors

Up to $1/4$ cup flour

Water

Inexpensive artists' paintbrushes

1 or 2 packets of small seeds, such as lettuce, carrot, beet, or radish seeds

A garden bed of any size

## HERE'S WHAT YOU'LL DO:

1. Cut your paper into strips about 1 inch wide and as long as your garden bed.

2. Mix flour and water until it has a pasty consistency.

3. Paint the flour paste down the center of your paper strip.

4. Press seeds into the paste, spacing them according to the directions on your seed packet or in a planting guide.

5. Place in a warm, dry area to let paste dry.

6. Once paste is dry, plant it in your garden. To plant your seed tape, simply dig a trench as deep as your seeds should go, lay the tape down, and cover it with soil. If the seeds require a planting depth of $1/4$ inch or less, simply place the tape on top of the soil and sprinkle a little soil on top.

## ALSO TRY THIS:

Instead of planting your seed tape, wrap it as a gift. To store seed tape, simply roll it up once it's dry and seal it in an airtight plastic bag. Then you can wrap it with ribbon or decorative paper, and top it with hand-written planting instructions.

# *The Living Canvas*

*This is what grew when Neli planted bulbs in a happy face design.*

**H**ave your kids draw a design in the soil. Plant seeds together and watch their design grow and change over time.

## HERE'S WHAT YOU'LL NEED:

Seeds suitable for furrow planting, such as carrot, beet, or spinach

A garden bed of any size

A planting guide

Access to water

## HERE'S WHAT YOU'LL DO:

1. Prepare your garden bed for planting.

2. Draw a design in the soil with your hand or a stick. You might make a spiral, a sun, or a picture of a goldfish, for example. Use the seed spacing information from your seed packets or planting guide to make sure there is enough space between your lines for your plants to grow.

3. Dig a furrow along the lines of your design to the appropriate planting depth for your seeds.

4. Sow your seeds in the furrow. For young kids, you can mix the seeds with sand to make furrow planting easier.

5. Cover your seeds with soil.

6. Keep your seeds watered and watch your design come to life.

## ALSO TRY THIS:

Plant bulbs, onion sets, or other plants in the shape of a kid-inspired design.

Paul Simon, children's garden expert at the National Gardening Association, captured his daughters doing some transplanting.

## Transplanting Seedlings into Larger Growing Areas

Transplanting seedlings is an immensely satisfying garden task for children. They start with a patch of bare soil and, in just minutes, turn it into a beautiful, growing bed of plants. At the same time, transplanting with young kids can be challenging insofar as seedlings are fragile, and children can inadvertently damage them. In order to improve your chances for success, give interested kids specific, age-appropriate tasks.

## Mapping the Bed

It works well to have kids map out where each plant will go in a bed prior to planting. Kids who are reading can use a planting guide or seed packet to find plant spacing information. Then they can use rulers or their farmer measurements to guide them. Once they know how far apart to plant their seedlings, children can use sticks or plant labels to mark where each plant should go. When they are finished, you can look at the bed and check the spacing before any plants go into the ground.

## Planting Seedlings

Once you have marked where each plant will go, it is time to dig in. Have very young children, who may damage the baby plants, dig the holes. Then you or an older child with more dexterity can remove a seedling from its container and place it in the hole. Explain and show them how to handle the plants gently in order to avoid damaging them. Then the young child can fill the hole in with soil. Life Lab's Education Coordinator, Amy Carlson, likes to tell her young daughter Greta that she is tucking the plant in, just like Amy tucks Greta in at night. This helps Greta remember to be gentle with the baby plant. Older kids can do the transplanting themselves, as long as you have first shown them how to remove the plants from their containers without damaging the stems or roots.

## *Keeping Things Growing*

We know it takes a lot of weeding, watering, and pest control to get to most kids' favorite part of gardening: the harvest. As Beth, a seasoned grandmother, explained, your caring for the garden behind the scenes will help your kids to taste success. This idea held true in every family garden we visited. The kids may have helped here and there with watering, weeding, and the like, but they were generally not the ones keeping the garden alive.

Nonetheless, garden maintenance provides a wealth of opportunity for kids to learn new skills, become adept with tools, and develop a sense of pride in their work. Therefore, although it may not cut down on your garden maintenance, involving your kids is well worth the effort. For example, 10-year-old West has his own oak tree in the garden. His mother, Tracy, has taught him how to use pruning tools, and West can prune it however he likes. By using adult tools and engaging in garden work alongside Tracy, West has developed a deeper sense of ownership and responsibility in the garden.

If your kids are interested in helping with garden maintenance, here are some ways they can get involved.

*Instant gratification comes from transplanting a little bit of life. • The right tool for the job makes a big difference.*

# *Bug Races*

Sow bug vs. sow bug, crossing the finish line.

**L**ook under rocks and dig in the soil to see what kinds of animals you can find. Then set up a Bug Race and watch how they move.

- - - - - - - - - - - - - - - - - - - - - - - - -

## HERE'S WHAT YOU'LL NEED:

1 clear jar

1 piece of paper or cardboard

1 magnifying glass

1 (6-foot) piece of yarn tied in a circle

## HERE'S WHAT YOU'LL DO:

1 While out in the garden, take a walk around and look for places insects might live. Check under rocks, in crevices, and on the undersides of leaves.

2 When you find a critter, take a minute to notice what it is doing. Is it sleeping, eating, or moving around? How does it move?

3 If you find a spider, leave it where it is and watch it in its habitat. For other critters, like ants, snails, beetles, and sow bugs, try to use your paper to coax the critter into your glass jar.

4 Once you've captured the critter, don't forget where you found it, because you'll want to return it to that exact spot.

5 Look at the critter closely with your magnifying glass. What is it like? How many legs does it have? Does it have wings? Can you see its eyes? Does it have antennae? How does it move? Does it walk, slither, hop, or fly?

6 To host a bug race, make sure you have at least 3 insects in your jar.

7 Take your insects to an open area. Place the yarn on the ground in a circle. Place the paper over the mouth of the jar, turn the jar upside down, and set it in the center of the yarn circle.

8 Remove the jar from over the bugs and watch them move. See which one gets out of the circle first.

9 Once the insects are out, use your jar to collect them back together and return each to his or her original home. If you have identified any pests, decide as a family how you wish to dispose of them.

⟶ CONTINUED FROM PAGE 94

a wonder to behold. In a magnificent magic trick of nature, once-living materials are decomposed and turned into a nutrient-rich soil amendment from which new life can bloom. By composting in the family garden, we can teach our kids about life cycles, encourage them to develop environmentally friendly habits, and treat our gardens to a free source of superb soil amendment.

Composting is a very kid-friendly gardening task. Kids of all ages can help gather materials from the garden and heap them onto the pile in layers. Once children are old enough to use adult-sized tools, they can chop materials with hand shears or spades and shape the pile with digging forks.

At Life Lab, we like to build whole compost piles with large groups of kids. We divide them into teams, including the Choppers, the Greens Team, the Browns Team, the Soil Team, the Water Team, and the Corner Monitors. The Choppers use hand shears to cut the green and brown materials. The Greens, Browns, and Soil Teams take turns layering their materials onto the pile. The Water Team dampens the pile with a hose after each layer is added and, after each layer has been added, the Corner Monitors use digging forks to push the sides in and pull the corners out, giving the pile a nice, square shape. Even with just a few kids, dividing up the tasks and assigning a few to each person or pair can make composting together a fun exercise in teamwork.

In the home garden, composting is often done by adding kitchen and garden scraps bit by bit over time. When taking this approach, be sure

2

*Who knows what you'll find in the compost pile?*

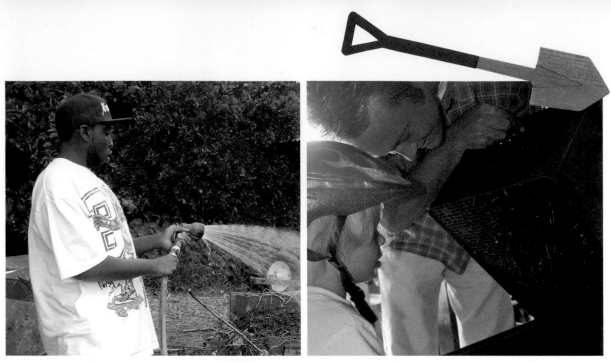

*Finishing off a pile, making it moist as a wrung-out sponge. • A stacking system worm bin makes for easy worm casting harvests.*

to have brown material such as sawdust, dried leaves, or straw on hand to cover up food scraps that might otherwise attract flies. Consider adding compost watering to your list of kid-friendly garden tasks as it is one task that young kids can easily master.

A worm bin composter can be maintained indoors with kitchen scraps throughout the year. Worm composting is also a favorite among children, many of whom come to regard their worms as pets. Charlie, a lively 4-year-old boy, loves feeding his worms; composting has already become a way of life for him. When he sees a banana peel in a parking lot, he tells his parents, "That needs to get composted."

Kids of all ages can help with starting and maintaining a worm bin. They can shred newspaper for bedding, collect food scraps for the worms, deliver food to their worms, and bury food in the bedding. Collecting food scraps for a worm bin provides a wonderful opportunity to help kids understand where food comes from. Explain to your children that you will be feeding the worms food that came from plants. Then, at the end of a meal, you can ask them, "Which of these foods comes from plants? Did the lettuce come from a plant? How about the chicken bone? Yogurt? Bread?" In sorting appropriate food for your worms, you may find the chance to teach your kids that bread comes from wheat, sugar from sugar cane, or tofu from soybeans. It can be fun to look for pictures of these plants growing or to plant a few in the garden, just to help kids get a complete picture of where our everyday foods come from.

Sifting the compost is also a very kid-friendly task. You can sift through finished compost by hand or with a sifter.

We use two kinds of sifters. One is a piece of

hardware cloth stapled into a frame made of 2 × 2s. The other, simpler version is a small-holed nursery tray. Kids pile finished compost on the tray and shake it over a bucket or tarp. Generally, the finished compost or worm castings fall through, and the material that needs more time to decompose stays on top. Most, but not all, worms and other decomposers also remain on top. Kids can then return the critters and materials that need more time to the compost pile or worm bin, and deliver the freshly harvested, finished compost or worm castings to a garden bed cleared for planting, or to a few of their favorite plants.

*Serious sifters use a wood-framed sifter with hardware cloth. • Small-holed nursery trays make great compost sifters.*

# The Disappearing Act: Observing Decomposition

*A compost bag teaches what will rot and what will not.*

In a small science experiment, have your kids pile soil and various ingredients into a large bag. Have them predict what will happen to the mixture over time, and then observe to test their predictions.

## HERE'S WHAT YOU'LL DO:

1 Gather organic and inorganic materials with which you are ready to part.

2 Have a look at all of the ingredients gathered and discuss the order in which you think they will decompose. Write down your predictions.

3 Mix all of your ingredients in a plastic bag. Leave space at the top for air, and then seal the top of the bag.

4 Tape your predictions to the outside of the bag, and set it outdoors in a sunny location.

5 Return to your bag each week to open it and allow the air to circulate a bit.

6 After about a month, dump the contents of your bag and see which of your items decomposed completely, partially, or not at all.

## HERE'S WHAT YOU'LL NEED:

- 1 large, plastic bag
- 1 bucket full of damp soil
- Various organic materials, such as yard trimmings and plant-based kitchen scraps
- Various inorganic materials, such as old plastic cups, metal coins, or pages from a newspaper or magazine

## ALSO TRY THIS:

If you are ever curious about how quickly something decomposes, just add it to your compost pile or bury it in the soil. You may be surprised by how long a so-called bio-degradable plastic cup, for example, lasts in the pile. Be sure to sift these test items out before adding finished compost to your garden beds.

# Worm Bin Bingo

In this game, two or more players search through worm compost for various critters, and try to line up three in a row on a bingo card. You can download a set of Worm Bin Bingo cards at lifelab.org/worm-bingo.

## HERE'S WHAT YOU'LL NEED:

1 Worm Bin Bingo card per player

1 shovelful of contents from an active worm bin

Newspaper

Sticks, old spoons, or other objects for digging around through the worm bin contents

Beans or other objects for marking boxes on the bingo card

## HERE'S WHAT YOU'LL DO:

1 If this is new to your kids, dump a shovelful of worm bin contents onto a piece of newspaper and show them how to move and handle worms and other critters carefully, without harming them.

2 Give every player a bingo card.

3 Place a large scoop of worm bin contents on a piece of newspaper in the center of the group.

4 Have the children search through the worm bin

contents for the critters on their cards. When they find one, have them show you and then mark it with a bean on their card.

5 Whoever fills a line across their bingo card first calls out "Bingo!" and wins the game.

## ALSO TRY THIS:

Use this game as a jumping off point for looking carefully at the diversity of life in your bin. Once someone has won the game, see if you can work as a team to find all of the critters on your cards. As you are working together on this task, take time to look carefully at the characteristics of the animals. Ask your kids leading questions to encourage detailed observation: "Can you see inside the worm egg? Can you tell which foods the sow bugs like best?"

*Worm Bin Bingo card set available to download at lifelab.org/worm-bingo.*

*Edible theme beds,
like a pizza bed,
connect gardening
with what we eat.*

**Chapter 3**

# Pizza Pies 🍕 and Pumpkin Jungles

## THEME GARDENS

SNEAK PEEK: Cornhusk dolls–or action figures •
Creating a butterfly buffet • Crunch-n-munch beds •
Zoo beds • and more

Beth and granddaughters have a snapdragon chat.

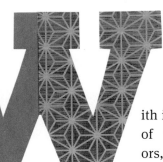

**W**ith its wide array of plants of various shapes, colors, and sizes, the spiral-shaped bed in the center of our Life Lab Garden Classroom inevitably draws the attention of all our young visitors. We often find children smelling the catnip, rubbing the soft lamb's ear and fuzzy kangaroo paw flowers, or staring down a bat-face cuphea. "What do all these plants have in common?" we ask. With signs naming each plant, the children soon begin to realize that every plant in this bed has an animal name. It's a zoo bed!

On a production farm, you might see acres and acres planted in the same crop. Part of the charm of a home garden, however, is the great variety of plants packed into a small space. In a family garden, this biodiversity not only allows the gardener to grow a variety of crops for the kitchen; it also provides a wide range of sights, smells, textures, and tastes for kids to explore.

Many gardeners working with children arrange their gardens into kid-friendly themes. In Life Lab's Garden Classroom, for example, we have a pizza bed, where we grow ingredients necessary for making a pizza; a tops and bottoms bed, with plants featured in Janet Stevens's storybook, *Tops and Bottoms*; adaptation beds, with plants adapted to live in unique habitats; a pollinator bed, with plants that attract bees, butterflies, and other pollinators; and an herbs of the world bed. There are so many ideas for theme beds—our suggestions are by no means exhaustive but may prove a useful jumping-off point as you and your kids brainstorm themes for your garden. If you want to explore even more theme garden ideas, browse the website of Michigan's 4-H Children's Garden (4hgarden.msu.edu/kidstour/tour.html) and take a look at more than 50 themed garden areas.

Of course, the best source of ideas for engaging your kids in your garden will be, well, your kids. Children know what they love, and they rarely hesitate to share what they are into with the rest of us. Look for opportunities to incorporate what they like into a Favorites Bed in your garden. You might have a bed of all pink plants, a prehistoric bed filled with plastic dinosaurs and prehistoric-looking plants, or a bed with plants growing out of pirate ships or pirate hats.

## Breakfast or Lunch or Dinner in Bed

A great way to help kids make the connection from soil to supper is by planting all of the ingredients for a meal in a single garden bed. As you and your kids tend to the crops, you can talk about the meal in store. Imagine the excitement of eating a soup that your kids helped prepare, not only all day, but all season. While you wait to harvest, prepare, and enjoy your meal, you and your kids will almost be able to *taste* the anticipation.

> **PROJECT**
>
> # Planting a Pizza Bed
>
> "Who thinks pizza grows in the ground?" we ask children as they circle around our pizza bed. In this circular garden bed, the circumference, or crust, is planted in wheat, and the slices are full of plants for pizza toppings. Depending on the season, children may find tomatoes, peppers, and eggplant—or onions, garlic, artichokes, and spinach. As they brainstorm different pizza ingredients, we work together to trace the ingredients back to their source, and then look together for the corresponding plants. Of course, it wouldn't be pizza without the cheese, and so we have a wooden cow in one of the slices, and we've planted some oats for her to graze on. By the end of their visit, everyone can explain how pizza does indeed comes from the soil.
>
> *If you have less space than the 6-foot-diameter bed would require, you can plant all of these ingredients together in a smaller bed of any shape.*

## HERE'S WHAT YOU'LL NEED:

Finished, sifted compost

A shovel or digging fork

A circular garden space, at least 6 feet in diameter for a pizza-shaped bed

8 (1-foot) stakes

String

Scissors

Wheat seeds

Seasonally appropriate plants for pizza toppings, such as tomatoes, peppers, basil, eggplant, zucchini, onions, garlic, spinach, and herbs

Statues of a cow and a pig (optional)

## HERE'S WHAT YOU'LL DO:

1. Mark out your circle with a shovel, and then clear and prepare your garden bed.

2. Place a pair of stakes across from one another on the circle and tie the ends of a string to each stake, cutting your circle in half. Do this three more times, dividing your pizza into 8 equal sections, or slices.

3. Plant seeds and seedlings into each slice, following the spacing directions on the seed packets or planting guides.

4. Dig a furrow about 1 inch deep around the circumference of your bed. Sow wheat seeds around the edge to give the pizza a crust.

5. Water your bed regularly and watch your pizza grow.

## ALSO TRY THIS:

In addition to pizza beds, here are some other meal-themed beds that you and your family can plant together. If you want to harvest everything at once to make a meal, use the days until harvest guidelines to stagger your plantings. For example, if you want to make a salad with lettuce that takes 50 days and carrots that take 75 days, then plant the carrots 25 days before you plant the lettuce.

- *Salad bed:* beet, carrot, cucumber, lettuce, nasturtium, radish, spinach, sweet bell pepper, tomato

- *Stir fry bed:* Asian greens like bok choy or tatsoi, bunching onions, cabbage, chard, garlic, kale, snow pea, sweet bell pepper

- *Salsa bed:* cilantro, garlic, hot pepper, onion, sweet bell pepper, tomatillo, tomato

- *Soup bed:* garlic, green bean, greens like kale or chard, onion, shelling bean, sweet corn, potato, winter or summer squash

Searching for the ripest tomato.

# NOT ALL TOMATOES ARE CREATED EQUAL — OR RED

**MUCH TO THE** surprise and delight of young children, tomatoes come in a wide variety of shapes and colors. Look for colorful varieties such as 'Green Zebra', 'Yellow Pear', and 'Cherokee Purple', for example, to create a tomato rainbow in your garden. To ensure kid-friendly harvesting when growing a multi-hued tomato patch, plant varieties that ripen into different colors in separate areas. That way, you can tell your kids, "Any orange tomato in this bed is ripe, and any green tomato in this bed is ripe." If you are planting cherry tomatoes, which you should, think about planting in a place that's easy to access and harvest, so that you and your kids can snack the day away.

Supporting your tomato plant upright is a great way to save space and keep the fruit from rotting. You can purchase tomato cages or make your own trellises. One of the best trellises we have seen is made using 6 × 4-foot livestock fencing, with a minimum 4-inch grid spacing. Roll the fencing into a 4-foot tall cylinder around your tomato plant and stake the cylinder on two sides– you'll have a much better tomato cage than what you often find in stores.

## Tomato Harvest Celebration

One family we know hosts an annual tomato harvest party with their friends and neighbors. In the late summer, everyone brings tomatoes from their gardens and they make all sorts of treats. Salsas, sauces, Caprese salads, and roasted tomatoes are just a few items on the menu. They also have tomato tosses for the kids, and tomato still-life painting for all.

## One-Bite Salsa

Salsa ingredients don't come any better than this.

Grab a bag of tortilla chips and head out to the garden with your children. If you have a lemon tree, pick a lemon. Harvest an onion and mince it. Then you and your kids can take a tortilla chip and put some salsa ingredients on top: a cherry tomato, a small piece of onion, a sprig of cilantro, and a squeeze of lemon juice, for example. Arrange the ingredients on top of your chip and then use your teeth to blend as you enjoy a one-bite salsa.

## Growing a Three Sisters Garden

The Iroquois and many other Native American tribes traditionally planted corn, beans, and squash side by side. These crops grew so well together that they became known as the three sisters, and they remain a common intercrop in gardens today. The three sisters provide children with a wonderful example of interdependence. The corn stalks provide a trellis for the bean plants to climb; the beans, in turn, return nitrogen to the soil for the corn and squash; and the squash plants provide ground cover for the corn and beans. Children can learn a lot about cooperation by watching the three sisters grow together.

There are many ways to plant a three sisters garden. One method that works well in a home garden is to build a mound of soil. Plant your corn seeds first, in the center of the mound. Once the corn has grown to about 6 inches tall, plant pole bean seeds in a circle around the corn, and squash seeds along the sloping edges of the mound.

Kids appreciate instant gratification and, while all gardening requires patience, these plants all grow large and fast. This bed will give children a thrill as your mound becomes a densely packed jungle with plants climbing up and around one another.

*Corn, beans, and squash make a great growing team.*

3

# THREE Sisters STORYTELLING

**THERE ARE SOME** wonderful children's books about the three sisters growing together, as well as many stories online. If you plant a three sisters garden, consider reading some three sisters stories together. You can find a plethora of these stories and activities in the book *In the Three Sisters Garden* by JoAnne Dennee and in the online article *The Three Sisters: Exploring an Iroquois Garden*, free at the Cornell Garden-Based Learning website, blogs.cornell.edu/garden/.

# Cornhusk Dolls

Garden-grown dolls (aka action figures).

**HERE'S WHAT YOU'LL NEED:**

10 dry cornhusks

Handful of dry corn silks

Soaking bowl filled with water

Scissors

Thin string

Dried flowers and twigs

A felt tip pen (optional)

**HERE'S WHAT YOU'LL DO:**

1. Roll corn silks inside of a cornhusk to create the head.

2. Wrap 1 long husk over the head and tie below the head to form the neck. Allow the corn silks to stick out from each side, making hair.

3. Roll 2 husks together and tie them off at each end to create 1 long piece. Slip this piece under the neck to create arms. Now tie below this piece to hold the arms in place.

4. Cut a hole in a large husk to create a tunic. Slip this tunic over the head and tie it off at the waist.

5. Add skirt husks all around the waist and tie from below. Fold skirt husks down and add a sash along the top of the skirt to finish it off.

6. If you want to make pants instead of a skirt, divide the skirt in half and tie off each half along the bottom to form legs.

7. Decorate your doll however you like. You can draw on a face with a felt tip pen, add flowers to the hair and clothes, make tools from twigs, or do anything else you come up with.

You and your kids can use dry cornhusks, either from a three sisters garden or from a regular corn crop, to make dolls, animals, and even action figures. One mother and garden-based science teacher described the spontaneous creation of cornhusk action figures as her biggest garden craft surprise and joy. As imaginations were sparked, she would hear banter about corn ninjas, corn brides, and corn witches. Here was an activity that had delighted kids for hundreds of years, a solid part of our cultural heritage, still doing its magic today.

# SIMPLE STEPS TO CREATE
## YOUR OWN
# CORNHUSK DOLL

### 1. HEAD
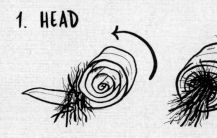

### 2. NECK

### 3. ARMS

### 4. TUNIC

### 5. SKIRT

### 6. PANTS

## 7. DECORATE & ENJOY !

**3**

*Homegrown for a floral fundraiser.*

## Sunflowers: Bright-faced Giants of the Garden

With their bright yellow petals, edible seeds, enormous stalks, and popularity among birds and insects, big sunflowers are a huge hit in family gardens.

PROJECT

# Growing a Sunflower House

What child doesn't love secret hideaways, forts, and playhouses? While we usually think of these as building projects, you and your kids can actually plant a simple, temporary sunflower house in your garden by growing sunflowers in a circle and tying the tops together. This will make a magical place for kids to spend time.

To grow a sunflower house, we recommend selecting a tall, sturdy variety of *Helianthus annuus,* such as 'Mammoth', 'Sunzilla', or 'American Giant'. You can intersperse these with smaller varieties of sunflowers or other flowers, so that when children are inside the sunflower house, they also have flowers to enjoy at eye level.

### HERE'S WHAT YOU'LL NEED:

**For seedlings:**

Seeds of the sunflower varieties you've chosen

Containers for starting seedlings indoors

Seed-starting mix

**For transplanted sunflowers:**

A garden space at least 8 feet in diameter

Finished, sifted compost

A shovel or digging fork

Access to water

Stepladder

Bailing twine

### HERE'S WHAT YOU'LL DO:

1. Start about 30 sunflower seeds indoors.

2. Once your seedlings are ready to be transplanted (when they have at least 4 true leaves), mark out a circle about 8 feet in diameter.

3. Prepare the soil and plant your seedlings about 1 foot apart, leaving about a 3-foot gap on one side, where your children will enter the house.

4. Water and weed your sunflowers, and watch them grow.

5. Once they are about 7 feet tall, you can start to tie your sunflowers together. You will probably need a stepladder.

6. Using bailing twine, tie a loose knot around a stem, about 1 foot below the flower itself. Pull gently across the circle and wrap your twine around a flower on the opposite side of the circle. Pull these flowers toward one another, allowing the flowering heads to cross. Then tie the stems together.

7. Continue like this until each flower is tied to another, across the circle.

## Roasted Sunflower Seeds

If you grew an edible seed variety of sunflower, don't forget to save some sunflower seeds for yourself. If you don't take the seeds, the birds and squirrels surely will.

Picking the seeds one by one out of the flower head might be all your family needs to enjoy the harvest. You can simply place the giant head on the kitchen table or somewhere else where you'd leave a snack bowl and watch the seeds disappear. But roasted seeds are a tasty treat, too. This is an easy recipe.

ACTIVE TIME: *45 minutes*

TOTAL TIME: *11 hours*

*1 large sunflower head yields 2–3 cups of seeds*

### Here's what you'll need:

*1 or more large, dry sunflower heads*
*Large paper bag*
*Gloves*
*Hardware cloth screen*
*Mixture of ⅓ cup salt per 2 quarts water*
*Baking sheet*
*Airtight container*

### Here's what you'll do:

❶ Watch your sunflower for when it's time save the seeds. The petals will drop, the backside of your sunflower head will turn yellow and dry, and the seeds in the middle of the flower should be fully developed.

❷ If you have competition (from birds or squirrels) for these seedy snacks, cover your flower head with a large paper bag until the dried head is ready to be harvested. If the bag gets moist, change it out to prevent mold growth.

❸ Once the flower head is fully dry and brown on the backside, cut the stem and store the flower head in a warm, dry place where critters cannot eat it.

❹ If it is truly dry, getting the seeds from the head should be fairly easy: just rub or pick them out. You might want to wear gloves since many parts of the dried sunflower can be prickly.

❺ If you are processing many sunflower heads at once, try rubbing the face of the dried flower on a ½-inch hardware cloth screen to speed up the seed removal process.

❻ Cover unshelled seeds overnight with a salt mixture of ⅓ cup salt per 2 quarts of water.

❼ Drain the seeds and pat dry.

❽ Place evenly on a baking sheet and bake at 300 degrees Fahrenheit, stirring occasionally, for about 30 minutes or until golden brown.

❾ Cool and store in an airtight container (if they make it that long).

### Also try this:

Experiment with different types of seasoning like chili powder, tamari, or Cajun spice.

## Natural Bird Feeders

As your sunflower heads dry, the seeds will loosen. You and your kids can pull out some seeds to make happy faces or other designs with the flower heads. You can also leave the dry flower heads standing in your garden and watch as birds begin to congregate and eat the seeds right out of the flower head.

## Cook's Confetti: Edible Flowers

Edible flowers allow us to bring the beauty of the garden into the kitchen, adding rich colors to salads, entrees, and even beverages. You may choose to plant edible flowers all together in a single bed or intersperse them throughout your garden. Consult a local garden center or planting guide to find varieties that will thrive in your area. A fun challenge can be to seek out an edible flower in every color of the rainbow, or varieties that bloom in various seasons. Your kids will delight in contributing to family meals by sprinkling the petals over salads, into pitchers of water, or along the edges of plates.

# A PALATE FOR POSIES: safe edible flowers

*These edible floral jewels were picked by little fingers.*

EDIBLE BLOSSOMS are often used as a decorative garnish. When introducing them into a young child's diet, choose only flowers that you have grown, as you don't know what has been sprayed on store-bought bouquets. Watch carefully the first time you or your child tries a new kind–flower petals, like other new foods, can cause allergic reactions. Remind your kids that not all flowers are edible, so before eating any flower out of the garden, they should show it to you first. Eat only the petals of the flower, and sample in moderation. Here are a few blossoms that are safe and fun to nibble.

**Red:** bachelor button, carnation, daylily, nasturtium, scabiosa
**Orange:** calendula, carnation, daylily, marigold, nasturtium
**Yellow:** calendula, carnation, daylily, marigold, nasturtium, viola
**Green:** broccoli (flower bud)
**Blue/Purple:** bachelor button, borage, chive, daylily, garlic, lavender, onion, viola
**White:** bachelor button, carnation, cauliflower (flower bud), chamomile, citrus, daylily, garlic, mints, onion, pineapple guava, stock

## Decorative Ice Cubes

*Filling ice trays with flower petals and water is a fun job.*

You can use edible flower petals and mints to make fanciful ice cubes for any festive occasion. Fill an ice cube tray halfway up with water and freeze. Then collect colorful, edible flowers and place a single petal on top of each ice cube. Pour a thin layer of water over the petals and freeze again, this time locking the petals into the ice cubes. These flower cubes are beautiful in glasses of water, or placed together in a large bucket with beverages at a birthday party or other event.

## Cut Flower Rainbow Bed

Did you know that the color of a flower often determines which pollinators will visit it? White flowers, for example, are often pollinated by nocturnal insects, such as moths. Their light color makes them easier to spot in the dark. Red flowers, on the other hand, are often pollinated by hummingbirds. By planting a wide range of flowers in your garden, you and your children will not only fill your garden with various colors to enjoy, draw, and use in bouquets and other garden art projects—you will also invite a diverse group of pollinators and other beneficial insects into your garden, creating exciting wildlife viewing opportunities for all visitors.

Cut flower gardens are wonderful areas for children to explore harvesting, because the more flowers that are cut, the more will grow. A good rule of thumb is to cut at the base of the flower stem. This makes for nice bouquets and leaves the plant looking tidy. Ideally, flowers should be cut in the early morning before the heat of day, with stems placed in a bucket or vase of water as soon as possible. If a plant has spent flowers, remove those dead heads. Deadheading is a great garden task for kids to take on throughout the year.

In addition to cut flowers, you and your children can also create other rainbows in your garden. An edible rainbow bed in the summer, for example, might include red bell peppers, orange cherry tomatoes, yellow summer squash, green beans, and purple eggplant. In the fall, you might plant red beets, orange carrots, yellow-stemmed chard, green lettuce, and purple kohlrabi or kale.

*Bouquet-making can be a great party activity.*

### Growing a Rainbow of Cut Flowers

Plan your rainbow flower garden by identifying cut flowers of each color that thrive in your region and bloom during the same general time frame. We've listed suggestions, but you will need to consult a local garden center or planting guide for regional specifics. Once you have selected flowers for each color, you can prepare a bed for planting. You and your kids may choose to plant your rainbow in a traditional rectangular garden bed or, if space permits, you may choose to plant it in the shape of an actual rainbow.

# SUMMER BLOOMING CUT FLOWERS BY COLOR

| Red/Pink: | Orange: | Yellow: | Green: | Blue/Purple: | White: |
|---|---|---|---|---|---|
| amaranth, | coreopsis, | dahlia, | bells of | aster, | aster, |
| aster, | dahlia, | gladiolus, | Ireland, | bachelor | bachelor button, |
| cosmos, | gladiolus, | marigold, | gladiolus, | button, | bishop's lace, |
| dahlia, | marigold, | sunflower, | sweet annie, | nigella, | cosmos, |
| gladiolus, | sunflower, | rudbeckia, | zinnia | scabiosa, | dahlia, |
| nigella, | tithonia, | zinnia | | statice, | gladiolus, |
| scabiosa, | zinnia | | | veronica | nigella, |
| stock, | | | | | scabiosa, |
| zinnia | | | | | stock |
| | | | | | Shasta daisy |

## Flower Bling

In addition to bouquets, you and your kids can make flower bling, or jewelry. Head out to the garden with some 40-pound gauge fishing line, and cut flowers with sturdy centers, like daisies, black-eyed Susans, zinnias, or dahlias. Help your kids push the fishing line through the center of the flower. It should be sturdy enough that they won't need a needle. They can string as many flowers as they like onto the line. They may also want to add leaves or other soft garden items. To finish it off, tie the ends together to make bracelets, anklets, crowns, necklaces, or whatever else they can come up with.

*Blooming necklaces make great flower bling.*

# Gathering a Bountiful Bouquet

It is no wonder that fresh flower bouquets are classic gifts and decorations. Bouquets allow us to bring the brilliant colors and scents from the garden into our homes. A hand-picked bouquet also communicates to our friends and family that we were thinking of them. Some gardening parents keep a fresh bouquet in their kids' rooms at all times. We imagine that coming home from school to find a fresh bouquet in one's room reminds a child that someone loves them, and thought of them while they were away.

Kids of all ages will delight in helping make bouquets by choosing, cutting, and arranging flowers. Happily, there is no wrong way to build a bouquet. This is one way to do it.

**HERE'S WHAT YOU'LL NEED:**

Garden shears

Gathering basket or container for cut flowers

Vase or jar to hold bouquet

Water

**HERE'S WHAT YOU'LL DO:**

1. Cut flowers in the early morning if possible, before the heat of the day. Have children choose big, tall flowers for the center of the bouquet. Cut at the base of the flower stem.

2. Gather some medium-sized flowers that they think look nice surrounding the big flowers. They can even hold the big flowers up next to other flowers to test out the combinations.

3. Surround the bouquet with the smallest flowers, grasses, ferns, or anything else that fills the spaces in and around the bouquet.

4. When your kids are happy with the appearance of their bouquet, cut stem bottoms so that they are all even.

5. Place the flowers in a vase or jar of water. Kids can set their bouquets somewhere special to them: maybe on the kitchen table, a windowsill in the den, or the desk in their room.

*Must munch much milkweed to metamorphose.*

## *Attracting Butterflies to Your Garden*

Butterflies fascinate children. From their amazing life cycle to the mesmerizing patterns on their wings, butterflies give us so much to look at and enjoy. You and your kids can attract butterflies into your garden by planting perennial plants that butterflies use for food or shelter. Then, when the butterflies visit, you will have ample opportunities to explore them together. A wonderful challenge for a child of any age is to see if they can sit perfectly still next to a butterfly until it lands on them.

## Creating a Butterfly Buffet

As we know, butterflies have different stages of life and therefore different needs when it comes to the plants on which they depend. You and your kids can plant beds or areas that are tailored to the needs of butterflies at their different life stages, then observe what happens during that stage.

A wonderful way to experience the butterfly's life cycle firsthand with your kids is to raise your own butterflies. Of course, different regions have different varieties of butterflies, and the method of raising them will be determined by the variety you choose. For a wonderfully user-friendly, visual introduction to raising butterflies, including species selection, appropriate food and habitat provisions, and more, visit raisingbutterflies.org/getting_started.

# PLANTS for the STAGES of a BUTTERFLY'S LIFE

**LARVAL STAGE:**
ceanothus
common fennel
currants and gooseberries
lavatera
lupine
milkweed
passion vine
penstemon
toadflax
veronica
yarrow

**ADULT STAGE:**
aster
borage
butterfly bush
columbine
coreopsis
heliotropes
lantana
lavender
marigold
oregano
rosemary
Shasta daisy
sweet alyssum
yarrow

Make an ordinary drink fancy with herbal infusions.

## Nature's Pantry and Pharmacy: Culinary and Medicinal Herbs

Herbs pique children's interest by appealing to their senses. Young kids love to run their hands along the tops of leaves and then smell the scents left, to freshen their breaths by chewing on a cool mint leaf, or to enjoy a hot tea flavored with herbs they themselves collected. Because many herbs are perennial, they also provide us with garden activities and beauty throughout the year, even when many of our beds may be bare. Finally, growing culinary and medicinal herbs gives

## COMMON MEDICINAL HERBS FOR HOME GARDENS

| PLANT | USE | PREPARATION |
|---|---|---|
| *Calendula* | Soothes skin; helps wounds heal | Salve |
| *Chamomile* | Soothes stomach aches; soothes skin | Tea made from flowers; salve |
| *Comfrey* | Soothes bruises and sprains | Applied externally as poultice |
| *Horehound* | Provides respiratory relief | Chopped and mixed in spoonful of honey |
| *Lavender* | Soothes skin; calming fragrance | Salve; use with bath salts |
| *Lemon Balm* | Strengthens immune system; relieves headaches; adds flavor to other teas | Tea made from leaves |
| *Peppermint* | Calms upset stomach and relieves flatulence; clears nasal and sinus congestion | Tea made from leaves; inhaled as vapor |
| *Sage* | Provides respiratory relief for congestion, cough, sore throat | Tea made from leaves; throat gargle |

children firsthand experience with the variety of ways people use plants to enrich their lives.

Of all the garden plants we grow, herbs are some of the easiest. Most common culinary herbs are perennials, and some of the annual varieties—like dill and chamomile—reseed so well you might think they are perennials. Some, like mints (which kids love), are very hardy and just keep spreading. You could consider planting mints in a container to keep them in check. Most prefer full sun and good drainage, and are well suited to container growing.

## Sun Tea

The idea of solar energy becomes real to kids when they can use it to make tea in the garden. Sun tea is a wonderful, kid-friendly garden treat for a sunny day. Find a quart-sized glass jar, clean it thoroughly, and then fill it with water. Walk around the garden with your children and have them add five sprigs of the herbs of their choice. Some nice options include lemon balm, mint, and chamomile. If you are collecting herbs with very young children, you can snip the sprigs and then let them tear the leaves off. Older children can snip the sprigs themselves. Once you have added the herbs, seal the jar and set it in the direct sunlight. Within a few hours, the flavor from the herbs should have infused the water. Serve the tea warm, or pour it over ice for a cool beverage on a hot day. On a cloudy day, you can also use garden herbs to make a hot tea.

## Homemade Tea Bags

You and your kids can make tea bags with dried chamomile, lemon balm, peppermint, mint, or other herbal tea plants growing in your garden. Simply harvest the herbs and hang them upside down in a warm, dry place until they are dehydrated. This will usually take about 2 weeks. Then you and your kids can crumble the dried herbs onto clean coffee filters, and tie each one into a bundle with a string. Label your tea bags, either by tying paper tags to each string, or by placing all of the bags into boxes and labeling and decorating the boxes.

You can also mix a few herbs together before making the tea bags, for a garden medley tea. A fun way to do this with kids is to have them close their eyes and smell various combinations of herbs to decide which combinations smell the best together. Or they can make combinations for you to smell while you close your eyes. In addition to creating delicious garden teas, you and your kids are also enjoying a sensory garden experience.

3

## Have a Tea Party

As long as you and your kids are making teas, why not invite some friends over for a tea party? You can set up a table and chairs indoors or out, decorate with fresh flowers and other garden-fresh items, and enjoy your garden tea together. Tea parties give us a great opportunity to explore our theatrical sides. At a garden-based summer camp in California, garden tea parties became a tradition. Kids would all harvest herbs and add them to the boiling water. While the tea was steeping, they would decorate a little table and chairs in the garden, and then don costumes from the costume trunk. Once the tea was served, it was traditional for everyone to speak in boisterous British accents and clink cups frequently until the party wound down.

## Soothing Salves

It's always fun to introduce children to nature's pharmacy in the garden. We show them plants for healing cuts, settling upset stomachs, soothing sunburns, or cooling the itch left by poison oak. This knowledge then comes to life for kids when we incorporate medicinal herbs from our garden into balms, salves, and the like. Furthermore, salves made with herbs from the garden make delightful gifts for family and friends. When making salve, young children can contribute by harvesting and drying garden herbs, stirring the ingredients, and decorating the containers. Older children can also help with heating, testing, and adjusting the recipe as needed to obtain an ideal consistency.

Homemade salve and lip balm require many helping hands.

Salves and balms are really the same thing. So you and your kids can make personalized gifts for friends and family, using the same recipe, simply by choosing different containers, or by customizing labels—Batter's Balm for a baseball player, or Gardening Grammy's Hand Salve for a grandmother with a green thumb.

# Making Julie's Lavender Belly Balm

Former Life Lab staffer Julie Grinvalsky was known to be particularly talented with homemade treasures, including a belly balm she gave as a gift to expectant mothers. Making her soft, soothing balm requires a little pre-preparation, but it's well worth the effort.

At least a month prior to making your balm, harvest and dry a handful of lavender stalks. To do this, simply snip the stalks and bundle them together. Hang your flowers upside down in a warm, dry place for at least 2 weeks. Once dry, brush the flowers from the stalk and, if you are not using them right away, store in an airtight container. Then, at least 2 weeks prior to making your salve, mix 1/4 cup dried lavender flowers with 1/2 cup organic, cold-pressed extra virgin olive oil in a clean, dry, pint-sized mason jar. Leave in a dark, warm indoor place for 2 weeks, allowing the lavender to infuse the oil. Now you are ready to make your balm.

*It can be very difficult to get the wax off of items once you make balm with them, so it is best to use old things that you will use only for making balms. Thrift stores are a good place to find containers and old kitchen items that can be reused for making balm.*

## HERE'S WHAT YOU'LL NEED:

- 3 metal teaspoons
- Small saucepan
- Water
- Stove
- 1/2 cup lavender-infused olive oil, prepared ahead of time
- Cheesecloth
- 1 empty glass jar
- 4 tablespoons grated or chunked beeswax
- 3 tablespoons cocoa butter, grated or chunked
- 10 drops lavender essential oil
- 12 small tins or jars

Chunked beeswax and cocoa butter are available at health food stores or via mail order; a good source is Mountain Rose Herbs, at mountainroseherbs.com, which also offers small tins or jars.

CONTINUED →

*Salves and balms can be used for hands or lips; purchase containers at an herbal medicine store or online.*

## HERE'S WHAT YOU'LL DO:

1. Place a few metal teaspoons in the freezer for later.

2. Strain your lavender-infused olive oil through cheesecloth and into an empty glass jar.

3. Compost the lavender bits.

4. Fill a small saucepan with a few inches of water and place over low heat on the stove.

5. Place your glass jar of lavender oil into the water while it is still cold, and allow the water and oil to heat together in this makeshift double boiler. The jar can break if the temperature changes too rapidly, so keep the heat on low.

6. Add the beeswax inside the jar and stir just until melted.

7. Using tongs, remove the jar from the saucepan.

8. Immediately add the cocoa butter, stirring it into the mixture and allowing it to melt. If the residual heat does not melt the cocoa butter completely, return the jar to the water until the cocoa butter is melted.

9. Now it's time to test the set of your balm. Take a spoon out of the freezer and pour a small drop of balm on the spoon. If it turns into a hard, smooth lump when you rub it, your balm is ready. If it is still too liquid-like, add a bit more cocoa butter to the jar, stirring to melt. Retest until the texture is to your liking. Occasionally, if heated too much, cocoa butter will give the balm a grainy texture. This is actually fine, as the grains will soften when rubbed into the skin.

10. Once the texture is to your liking, add 10 drops of lavender essential oil and stir to combine.

11. Pour balm slowly into tins or jars. You can let them sit overnight to harden, or you can carefully transfer them to the freezer where they'll set faster.

12. Decorate your containers with labels, stickers, raffia, dried lavender, and the like.

## ALSO TRY THIS:

Balms and salves work with all sorts of garden herbs. You and your kids can walk your garden and harvest any edible or medicinal herbs you find and create various salve combinations.

## Lavender Wands

A magic wand with super-herbal powers.

Lavender wands are wonderful, whimsical crafts that children of all ages can help make. Simply harvest five sprigs of lavender with flexible stems. Tie the stalks together with a thin, pretty ribbon at the base of the flowers, leaving one end of the ribbon long. Now turn the flowers upside down and bend the stems back over the ribbon knot. Take the long end of the ribbon and weave through the lavender stems, going over then under each one. Once your woven stems cover the entire flower heads, tie them together to form a lavender wand.

⌐ PROJECT ¬

# Lavender Bath Salts

**L**avender bath salts are easy to blend, and they make wonderful gifts for friends, family, and anyone you want to acknowledge for their hard work, such as teachers, farmers, or parents.

### HERE'S WHAT YOU'LL NEED:

1 cup Epsom salts

1 cup sea salt

2 tablespoons baking soda

10 drops lavender essential oil

Handful of dried lavender buds

Large bowl

### HERE'S WHAT YOU'LL DO:

1 Stir everything together in the bowl.

2 Scoop some of the mixture into small bags or jars.

3 Decorate with labels and ribbons. Your label might include some directions, like "Add several tablespoons of these bath salts to a warm bath and take a well-deserved soak."

3

*There's nothing like a lemon cuke for garden snacking.*

## Crunch-n-Munch Beds

A mother of a 2-year-old told us that her summer garden goal was to create "an edible food forest" for her daughter, a place where every plant her daughter encountered would be thorn-free and edible without cooking. She envisioned a sort of jungle where her daughter could wander through, picking and eating as she went. Indeed, children of all ages love eating foods fresh from the vine. In fact, another mother told us that her 4-year-old son would not eat green beans, carrots, or peas at all in the house, but he would harvest and eat basketfuls out in the garden.

## FREE FOOD

A 5-year-old said that her favorite thing in the garden was all the "free food." Here is a short list of just the kinds of plants she was talking about—the ones kids can pick, wash, and eat without any further preparation.

| | | | |
|---|---|---|---|
| apples | celery | mint | peppers |
| berries | cherry tomatoes | melons | plums |
| broccoli | corn | oranges | radish |
| carrots | figs | peaches | snow peas |
| | green beans | | sugar snap peas |
| | lemon cucumbers | | |

## Carnivorous Plants—or, the Case of the Blood-Sucking Bog

Kids are inherently fascinated by anomalies. Just think about how they react when they see a 4-leafed clover or identical triplets, for example. As they construct their view of how the world works, these unique sightings thrill them. Carnivorous plants seem to fall into this category. While most plants make their food from sunlight via photosynthesis, this small group of plants supplements their diet with nutrients from insects. And in order to do this, they have to *hunt*. Kids will watch for hours on end to see how a plant attracts and traps its prey. They will count the daily catch. And in the process, they will learn a surprising amount about the adaptive features of these amazing plants.

You might be surprised to know that carnivorous plants grow all over the world. They are usually found in bog-like environments, which you can replicate at home. Californiacarnivores.com is the largest carnivorous plant shop in the United States. Growing these fascinating plants isn't difficult, but there are a few secrets that will increase your chances of success.

Use a plastic or glazed ceramic pot to help retain moisture in your soil mix. Make sure the pots have drainage holes. Use a soil mix of horticultural grade sand, perlite, and sphagnum peat moss. There are lots of types of peat moss available, so make sure to get sphagnum, which give carnivorous plants the acidity they need. Water with distilled, reverse-osmosis, or pure rainwater. These plants do not succeed if watered with domestic water that has high mineral content. Finally, place your pot in a deep tray filled with the same pure water so your plant will always be moist.

Since these plants grow in a low-nutrient environment, which is one reason they evolved to digest animals, they do not need much or any fertilization. If you do fertilize, sprinkle lightly with Max-Sea fertilizer applied monthly at a ratio of ¾ teaspoon per gallon of water.

Clearly, carnivorous plants require specific care, but it is well worth it since kids love having a flesh-eating plant to call their own. Each species is a bit different and you can find indoor and outdoor varieties, so make sure to read up on specific care instructions to keep your critter-eating plant thriving.

*Staring down a pitcher plant.*

## Getting Close to Your Carnivore—But Not Too Close

One of the most fun things to do with carnivorous plants is just to study them carefully and try to figure out how they work. Together with your child, look carefully at each plant. How does the plant attract insects? What kind of insects does it trap? How does the plant keep the insects there once they land? Have your child look, smell, and feel the plant for sweet nectar, sticky walls, spiny traps, and other structures that help it capture insects. Then draw the plants together, including all of the detailed features you see. You can label these parts, and even give them names, such as "delicious sweet pool of nectar," or "spiny gates."

After looking carefully at carnivorous plants together, you and your kids can design your own carnivorous plants. Using art supplies, you can draw or build models of plants with various imaginative structures that would aid them in capturing prey.

*Going deep for the spud-planting in furrows yields more taters.*

## Potatoes as Buried Treasure

Potatoes make a fantastic addition to any family garden for several reasons. Kids will be fascinated when they see that you can grow potatoes from other potatoes. Potatoes also provide a very high edible yield per square foot, a yield which can be cooked up into so many tasty meals. And there is something positively magical for kids about digging potatoes out of the ground. Squeals are guaranteed as your kids hunt around in the soil for buried treasure. They will often search every corner of a potato patch to make sure they have not left any in the ground. Of course, if they did, they will know the following spring when those plants start to grow again.

# Growing Potatoes in Pots

A tower of potatoes.

**G**rowing potatoes in a container is fun and saves space. We have seen potatoes grown in large reused plant containers, in wire fencing staked in the ground, and even in chicken feed bags. You might have heard of growing taters in tires, but the jury is still out on the toxicity of tires, so we would opt for another method.

## HERE'S WHAT YOU'LL NEED:

Amended soil

Straw (optional, for later)

Seed potatoes

Container no less than 18 inches in diameter, with drainage

## HERE'S WHAT YOU'LL DO:

1. Fill the bottom of your container with about 6 inches of amended soil.

2. Place your seed potatoes 6 inches apart on top of the soil, and bury with about 4 inches of soil.

3. Initially water gently. Overwatering can lead to rotting seed potatoes.

4. Once you see growth pop up, keep your container evenly moist but not wet. Containers can heat up and dry out quickly, so monitor moisture often.

5. Once your plants have about 8 inches of growth, it is time to add more soil. Or you can add a soil and straw mix, which will make pulling out young potatoes easier down the road. You just want to make sure that the mix you add will be able to stay moist and cover the leaves and stems below. This time, cover about two-thirds of the exposed plants.

6. As the plants continue to grow, repeat this process, covering stems and leaves to stimulate more potato tubers to grow.

7. Eventually your plants will flower. When they do, you can dig down and pull out some new potatoes.

8. You can also wait for the plants to die back, stop watering for about 2 weeks to let the potatoes cure, and then dump your container over, counting the jewels that emerge.

## Potato Pancakes

Kids tend to enjoy finger foods. Potato pancakes, or latkes, can be eaten with a fork and knife or by hand. Latkes are associated with traditional Eastern European Jewish cuisine, although similar fare exists in Ireland, Sweden, India, and Korea. They are especially delicious when topped with a dollop of sour cream and warm applesauce.

ACTIVE TIME: *45 minutes*  TOTAL TIME: *45 minutes*
*Makes 10–12 pancakes*

**Here's what you'll need:**

Enough potatoes to fill 2 cups when grated
1 onion
3 eggs
1 ½ tablespoons all-purpose flour
1 ¼ teaspoons salt
Cooking oil
Large frying pan

**Here's what you'll do:**

1. Grate 2 cups of potatoes.
2. Mince 1 tablespoon of onion.
3. Crack and beat 3 eggs.
4. Stir grated potatoes in with eggs.
5. Mix 1½ tablespoons flour and 1¼ teaspoon salt. Stir in with potatoes and eggs.
6. Stir in onion.
7. Heat cooking oil in skillet.
8. Use about 2 tablespoons of the potato mixture to create a pancake in the frying pan. Spread it out to about a 3-inch round. Cook until brown on a side, about 5 minutes. Then flip and cook until brown on the other side, approximately 5 more minutes.
9. Top with sour cream and warm applesauce or stewed apples or pears. Serve immediately.

### Potato Stamps

*Potatoes aren't the only food to make prints with.*

Older kids who are adept with X-Acto knives can use potatoes to make stamps. Younger children can draw designs that you can then carve into stamps for them to use. To make a potato stamp, simply slice a potato in half. Then, using an X-Acto knife, carve the flat surface of a potato half to make the shape you want for your stamp. Dip the raised design in a shallow dish of tempera paint or brush it on, and then press gently onto paper. You can use these potato stamps to create artwork, or to decorate wrapping paper, gift cards, or the like.

*Picking the perfect pumpkin.*

## *Pumpkin Jungle*

Even families who spend little to no time on farms or in gardens can often be found visiting pumpkin patches in the fall. From jack-o'-lanterns to pumpkin pie, these easy to grow giants from the squash family are a symbol of fall and lend themselves to all sorts of fun activities for children and adults alike.

## Growing Pumpkins

There are not many things you can grow in your garden that will be as big and prolific as a pumpkin vine. Make sure you have about an 8 × 8-foot space for these ramblers to spread out. If you are short on space, you can train the vines where you want them to go by carefully guiding them, even training them up a trellis or building. We saw a pumpkin fanatic who placed large nails up the side of his shed. These served as tendril holds and allowed him to train the vine to grow on the shed roof. He had to pick flowers off of the vertical vine so that the pumpkins wouldn't weigh them down.

Ideally, pumpkin seeds are planted directly in the ground when nighttime temperatures stay above 50 degrees, but if your growing season is short or your spring is cold and damp, you can choose to start your seeds indoors 3 weeks before your last frost. Pumpkins are heavy feeders, so add lots of compost and consider feeding throughout their growth with fish emulsion or another organic fertilizer. If you desire the perfect pumpkin, make sure that you sit it on its

## Pumpkin Leapfrog

What could be more fun for kids than playing leapfrog over big, orange pumpkins? To set up your course, harvest five or more pumpkins. Set them up in a row, each a few feet ahead of the last. Then play pumpkin leapfrog, and have young children use their hands to jump over each pumpkin. Don't forget to show them where the stem comes up so that they can make sure to not put their hand there. You can also set up a pumpkin slalom and have children weave back and forth between the pumpkins. This is a great party activity, and you can even make it a relay race with multiple teams.

## Personalize Your Pumpkin

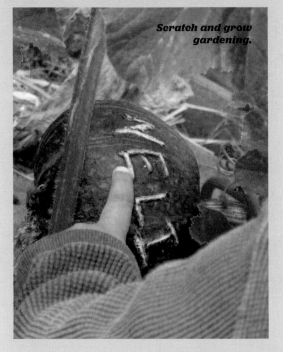

*Scratch and grow gardening.*

There are not many vegetables that you can write your name on, but you can with squash. When your green little pumpkin is about 3 to 4 weeks old and still on the vine, take a blunt, pointed object like a nail or ballpoint pen and etch in a word or drawing. No need to scratch in more than $1/8$ inch, just enough to break the skin. There will be a bit of residue, which you can wipe off. In the following weeks, you will see what you drew grow with the pumpkin.

## Soup Inside a Pumpkin

Imagine your child's delight when you take the lid off of a pumpkin and ladle a cup of soup from inside. Even the pickiest eater is likely to have some of this enticing soup or stew. To start, select a pumpkin that stands upright without wobbling. Wash the outside well, take the top off, and scoop out the seeds and strings. Brush the inside lightly with oil and bake the pumpkin at 350 degrees for an hour. While the pumpkin is baking, make the stew or soup of your choice. Pumpkin or winter squash soups are good options.

After an hour, check your baking pumpkin. When it is ready, the shell will be soft on the inside but still hard on the outside. At this point, remove the pumpkin from the oven. When your stew or soup is ready, pour it into your pumpkin shell. Stick a ladle inside and serve your soup fresh from the pumpkin. As you ladle out the soup, add a scoop of baked pumpkin to the top of each bowl. This is sure to be a hit at any fall gathering.

*A little pie guy learns the secrets to a flaky crust.*

bottom, which will allow it to grow evenly round. You can even place it on a board to reduce the chance of blemishes and rotting in wet soil.

## Easy Edible Fruit

Adding fruit trees or shrubs to a family garden is an exciting endeavor. Just think: most fruit trees planted when your children are babies will still be living there when your children grow up and leave home. Fruit also offer many opportunities for family activities. Do some comparative taste testing with different fruit, or varieties of the same fruit. Or preserve fruit for winter treats by dehydrating it or making fruit leathers and jams.

A new tree planted with your kids will grow with your family and most likely be woven into family traditions. In John's family, just such a

With help from a friend, straight from the tree to little Lee.

3

tradition has already been set with Neli's birthday. Peach pie is his birthday cake of choice.

## HOW MUCH SPACE DO YOU HAVE?

Some avocado trees can get to 50-plus feet, and not all backyards can afford to dedicate that much garden real estate, especially when you consider the shadow such a large tree will cast. Caring for and harvesting from such a tree can be difficult, to say the least. Look for dwarfing rootstock when purchasing fruit trees. Dwarfing rootstock and effective pruning can keep trees to a more manageable size.

## WHEN DO YOU WANT TO HARVEST YOUR FRUIT?

Look for early, midseason, or late varieties of the fruit you are selecting. For your family, it might make more sense to stagger the harvest dates of the trees you are planting for an early summer through fall harvest, rather than having all your fruit come on at once. Some trees even come with three or four varieties grafted on the same tree for an extended harvest. This is a great idea, but be aware that these trees often take a bit more pruning and maintenance.

## WILL MY TREE LIKE MY YARD?

We don't really know if trees have feelings, but we do know that they have needs, especially in relation to climate. For instance, some fruit trees, such as apples, need a certain number of chill hours below 45 degrees Fahrenheit to flower and fruit properly. The chill hours vary among varieties, so you should be able to select the tree that is right for your zone. Other trees, such as citrus,

cannot tolerate freezing temperatures. Some species of trees have been bred to be more cold tolerant and disease resistant, so research the temperature range and common diseases in your region and get what will work best for your yard. John selected a leaf curl-resistant peach tree for his yard, which has saved him time and effort from spraying to control the disease.

## WILL MY TREE FRUIT?

In order for a tree to produce fruit, it must be pollinated. This means that pollen must be carried (on bee's legs, butterfly whiskers, wind, or by some other mechanism) from a flower's anther to a flower's stigma. Some trees, such as sour cherries, are self-fruitful, which means that the anther and stigma needed for pollination are on the same variety, sometimes on the same tree, and sometimes even on the same flower. Most fruit trees, however, cannot self-pollinate, which means that they require cross-pollination from another tree in order to bear fruit. This information is usually listed on the plant label. If there isn't another tree that could provide pollination in your neighborhood, plant two trees to ensure a harvest.

For more information on fruit trees, see our Suggestions for Further Reading.

## *Zoo Bed*

A zoo bed is simply an area in your garden where every plant has an animal name. At Life Lab, kids love to look for the different ways that the zoo bed plants resemble their namesake animals. These plants also often lend themselves to sensory exploration, as in the soft leaves of a lamb's ear or the fuzzy flower of a kangaroo paw.

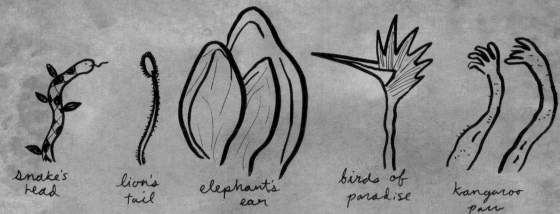

snake's head · lion's tail · elephant's ear · birds of paradise · kangaroo paw

# CHOICES FOR A ZOO BED

Not all plants that have animal references in their names have animal-like characteristics. The plants on this list all have obvious forms that resemble animals, and therefore they make great additions in any zoo bed.

**bat-face cuphea**
*(Cuphea llavea)*

**bird of paradise**
*(Strelitzia reginae)*

**chameleon plant**
*(Houttuynia cordata)*

**bear's breech**
*(Acanthus mollis)*

**lamb's ear**
*(Stachys byzantina)*

**elephant ear**
*(Colocasia species)*

**kangaroo paw**
*(Angiosanthos species)*

**lion's tail**
*(Leonotis leonurus)*

**snake's head**
*(Fritillaria meleagris)*

**tiger lily**
*(Lillium lancifolium)*

**turtlehead**
*(Chelone lyoni)*

**snapdragon**
*(Antirrhinum majus)*

**unicorn grass**
*(Juncus effuisus)*

## Using your Zoo Bed as an Imagination Station

The zoo bed is a space that really awakens the imagination. You and your kids might pick flowers and leaves from the plants and make a puppet show, with each plant representing its namesake animal. You can stick googly eyes on some to make them look even more like animals. Or you might place the plants along a pathway, and label them to make it look like a real zoo. Next to the lamb's ear, for example, you might have a sign welcoming visitors to the Lambs Petting Zoo, and inviting them to pet a lamb's ear. Some children even name their individual plants, as they would an animal.

## A Blindfolded Walk Through the Zoo

Since the zoo bed has plants with such a variety of textures and smells, it makes a great place to engage the senses. Of course, a great way to pique your other senses is to eliminate sight. For a fun, trust-building activity, walk around your zoo bed with your kids and make sure you all know the names of at least a handful of plants. Now you and your children can lead one another blindfolded to a single plant at a time. Have the blindfolded person feel it and then try to guess which plant they are visiting. If you would prefer to do this without a blindfold, you can also pick leaves or flowers from a handful of plants, put each into its own paper bag, and have each person feel the plant part to guess which plant it came from.

Nectar-rich ray and disc flowers attract pollinators.

# Chapter 4

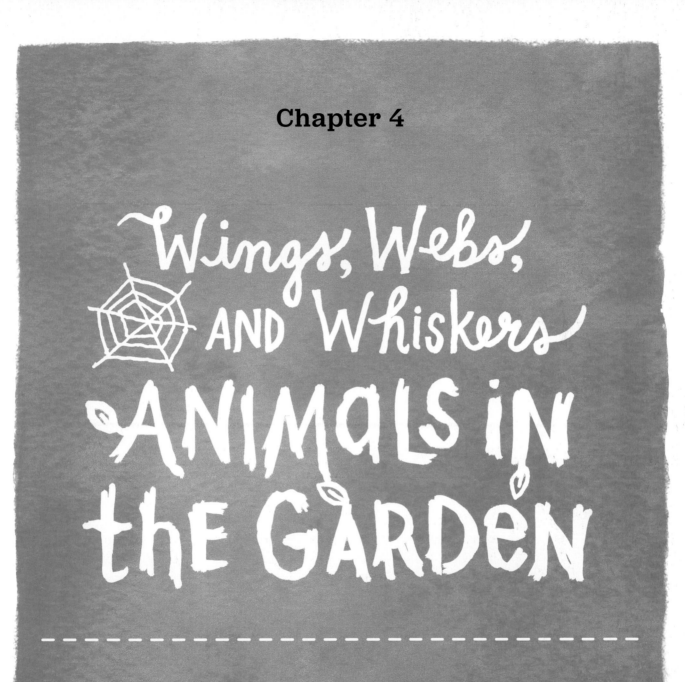

Wings, Webs, and Whiskers

ANIMALS IN the GARDEN

- - - - - - - - - - - - - - - - - - - - - - - - - - - - - - - - - -

**SNEAK PEEK: Making a bird blind • Building a barn owl box • Making a pond or bog for wild things • and more**

*A slithery garden visitor who also offers free gopher control.*

**A**t the end of every field trip to Life Lab's Garden Classroom, we ask kids to reflect on their favorite activities. Whether they have pressed apple cider; harvested, prepared, and eaten a hearty soup; ground corn into tortillas; or run like tractors through the field, the first highlights they mention inevitably seem to be the same: feeding the chickens; visiting the worms; and seeing the owls, bees, farm cats, salamanders, or any other animals they may have encountered. Over time we have realized that kids just love animals.

This is great news for a family gardener because, for better or worse—or, more accurately, for better *and* worse—thriving gardens are teeming with wildlife. As gardeners, we tend to be preoccupied with the gophers, squirrels, and insects that view our garden as a free buffet. In addition to these pests, however, there are scores of wild insects, birds, and other animals that keep our gardens growing. A healthy garden is, in fact, an ecosystem unto itself, within which you will find countless interactions between all of the plants and animals living there or just passing through. The worms and other decomposers, for instance, add nutrients to the soil as they decompose dead plant material. Bees, bats, birds, and butterflies pollinate the flowers, allowing plants to produce fruits, seeds, and, finally, new baby plants. Trees and other plants, in turn, provide shade, shelter, and food for many insects, birds, and other animals.

The trick, then, in gardening is to keep the pests at bay while welcoming helpful creatures for both garden health and family wildlife explorations. You can do something simple, such as placing a board on the ground to create a habitat for snakes and salamanders, or you may choose some more elaborate projects, such as building bird feeders or bat boxes, planting for wildlife, or installing a garden pond.

*Kids are attracted to all creatures, great and small.*

4

# Making Your Garden a Certified WILDLIFE HABITAT

**THE NATIONAL WILDLIFE** Foundation's Certified Wildlife Habitat program certifies gardens and open spaces as wildlife friendly. By making sure your garden meets certain criteria for wildlife, and paying a small fee, your garden can be listed with the NFW's registry of certified habitats. Your family will receive a certificate, a year's membership to the NWF, and tips to attract wildlife to your garden. So what does it mean to make your garden wildlife friendly? All you need to do is provide these key elements: food sources, such as native plants, seeds, and nectar plants; water sources such as a birdbath or pond; places for cover, such as a rock pile or birdhouse; and places to raise young, such as dense shrubs, a nesting box, or a pond. You will also need to establish sustainable gardening practices, such as mulching and fertilizing without chemicals. Learn how to be certified and much more on wildlife-friendly gardening at nfw. org in the United States, cwf-fcf.org/ in Canada, and wildaboutgardens.org/ in the United Kingdom.

*Make the right-sized hole for the right type of bird and you might end up with guests.*

4

What do you do when you catch a glimpse of a garden-friendly wild creature? We like to play up any and every such encounter. Before going out on a farm tour, we often teach kids how to walk stealthily and listen intently. We practice fox walking, which simply entails walking as quietly as possible. Then, as we get near the owl boxes or salamander boards, we have whole groups of kids fox walk, sometimes even on hands and knees, as they approach. If we see something, we silently burst with enthusiasm, pointing and miming at the baby owl or other creature.

Sometimes parents feel concerned that their child will ask, "What kind of bird is that?" and they will not know. This is a golden opportunity to teach kids about detailed observation and field guides. Even if you do know what kind of bird, insect, or other animal you have spotted, sometimes the best answer is, "I'm not sure. Let's see if we can find out." Then ask your child to look carefully. Ask as many questions as you can to keep them looking. For instance, "What colors do you see? How many legs does it have? Are there antennae? What is it eating? How is its beak shaped?"

After carefully observing the animal, look together in a field guide for a match. With young kids, an exact match is often difficult to find, but you can start with big differences. For example, after making detailed observations of a sparrow with your kids, you might open a bird field guide and show them the waterfowl. "Is it one of these? No? How can you tell?" Continue like this through some obvious mismatches. Whether or not you end up identifying the type of sparrow you found, your kids will remember more details from this encounter than if you had said, "Oh,

*Kids like catching animals; teach them to respect their garden friends.*

that's a house sparrow." In fact, in the spirit of observation, sometimes we skip the field guides altogether and just ask kids what they would name it. Children often come up with very creative and descriptive names, like the yellow-headed seedeater or the 6-legged fuzzy friend.

## Attracting Pollinators

Native plants have co-evolved over thousands of years with native creatures, so they are very well adapted to attract many beneficial insects. Disc and ray flowers, such as calendula, cosmos, rudbeckia, sunflowers, and zinnias also attract beneficial insects with their abundance of pollen. Other flowers have a broad floral structure that can act as a landing pad and insectary for various beneficial insects, like butterflies and wasps. Examples of these plants include buckwheat, dill, fennel, sweet alyssum, and yarrow.

If your climate allows it, plant perennials that bloom year-round. You can visit the Pollinator Partnership at pollinator.org to find a pollinator planting guide for your region. In Canada, refer to pollinationcanada.ca. In the United Kingdom, visit rhs.org.uk/Plants-for-pollinators.

## Attracting Amphibians and Reptiles

Leave some wild spaces for critters to hide or create some of your own. We often find salamanders in the dark, damp sections of our yards, especially underneath boards or planters. You can put out a sheet of plywood of any size and reptiles will likely take shelter underneath. Help your kids to remember to look under the boards, lifting and lowering them carefully, to find centipedes, worms, salamanders, beetles and more.

You can also create a rock pile for reptiles like lizards to lounge around and hide in. You can even make a toad abode by turning a ceramic flowerpot upside down. Prop one side up with a rock so the toad can get in and out, and place the abode in a shady spot near a water source.

## Attracting Birds

For all wildlife, of course, water is key. Try out a birdbath in your yard by placing a wide, shallow dish raised off the ground. If you have a large yard with trees, consider leaving dead trees standing or creating a brush pile to serve as roosting and foraging sites. You can also build or purchase nesting boxes and see if birds inhabit them. Different species of birds need different types of nest boxes. Consult Cornell's allaboutbirds.org website for nesting box designs and tips for your region. Finally, you can attract birds to your garden by increasing the number of bird-friendly plants or placing bird feeders around your garden.

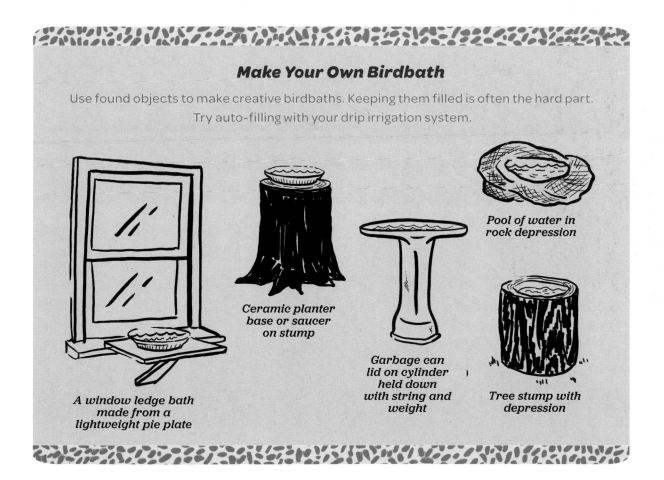

### Make Your Own Birdbath

Use found objects to make creative birdbaths. Keeping them filled is often the hard part. Try auto-filling with your drip irrigation system.

*Pool of water in rock depression*

*Ceramic planter base or saucer on stump*

*Garbage can lid on cylinder held down with string and weight*

*Tree stump with depression*

*A window ledge bath made from a lightweight pie plate*

# PLANTS TO Attract Birds

These plants will bring birds into your garden for you and your kids to enjoy.

**ANNUAL GARDEN PLANTS:**

amaranth
bachelor button
coreopsis
cosmos
seeding grasses
sunflower
tethonia
zinnia

**PERENNIAL GARDEN PLANTS:**

aster
butterfly bush
chrysanthemum
columbine
echinacea
goldenrod
scabiosa

**LARGER SHRUBS:**

bayberry
boxwood
currant
dogwood
elderberry
holly
honeysuckle
juniper
myrtle
rose
service berry
viburnum
yew

**PLANTS TO ATTRACT HUMMINGBIRDS:**

Typically hummingbirds like visiting red and orange tube-like flowers, but they don't limit themselves to only those.

azalea
bee balm
butterfly bush
coral bells
columbine
fuchsia
honeysuckle
lantana
lupine
penstemon
salvias
trumpet vine
weigela

*A little sunflower is a big meal for this acrobatic bird.*

## Homemade Bird Feeders

Feeding birds is a delightful way to observe wild-life in the garden. One easy way to do that is just to let large garden plants go to seed, creating natural feeders for birds. Installing man-made, store-bought, or simple homemade feeders will also bring the birds to you. John places bird feeders right outside the breakfast table window and, through the seasons, different types of birds entertain Neli while he feeds himself. Seeds, suet cakes (mixture of lard, seed, and fruits), mealworms, nectar, and fruit are examples of bird food.

### *Helpful bird-feeding tips:*

- Keep feeders away from areas where predators like cats can hide and ambush the birds.
- Place feeders at least 3 feet from windows, to avoid collisions.
- Feeders situated near large trees and shrubs often have more visitors.
- Keep seeds dry and watch for mold.
- Clean your feeders from time to time and let them dry completely before adding seed.
- Black oil sunflower seed in a tubular feeder is a great way to start, as it attracts many types of birds.
- Mix it up. Try different types of feeders and feed throughout the yard.
- Remember that many birds are migratory, so look for the right feed for the season's visitors.

Bird feeders come in all shapes and sizes, Visit birdfeeding.org for tips on feeders and feed, as well as a simple bird identification guides.

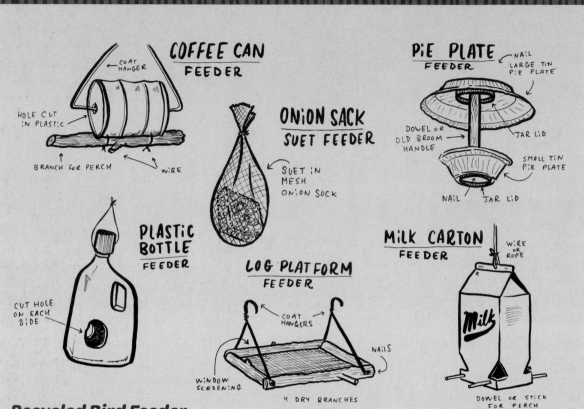

**COFFEE CAN FEEDER**

COAT HANGER

HOLE CUT IN PLASTIC

BRANCH FOR PERCH

WIRE

**ONION SACK SUET FEEDER**

SUET IN MESH ONION SOCK

**PIE PLATE FEEDER**

NAIL
LARGE TIN PIE PLATE

DOWEL OR OLD BROOM HANDLE

JAR LID

SMALL TIN PIE PLATE

NAIL   JAR LID

**PLASTIC BOTTLE FEEDER**

CUT HOLE ON EACH SIDE

**LOG PLATFORM FEEDER**

COAT HANGERS

NAILS

WINDOW SCREENING

4 DRY BRANCHES

**MILK CARTON FEEDER**

WIRE OR ROPE

Milk

DOWEL OR STICK FOR PERCH

## Recycled Bird Feeder

You and your kids can use an empty milk carton to make a bird feeder for your garden. To start, rinse your carton well and set it out to dry. Then, with an X-Acto knife, cut a 2-inch tall triangular hole near each of the bottom corners of the carton. Using a nail or other sharp object, puncture holes underneath the triangles. Push chopsticks through the holes, allowing them to stick out from both ends to create bird perches. Make a hole in the top of the milk carton and loop a piece of string through to hang your feeder. You and your kids may want to decorate the feeder with art supplies or with a collage of natural materials collected in the garden. Once it is decorated and ready to hang, fill the bottom of your carton with birdseed, hang it from a tree or fence in your garden, and watch for winged visitors.

We've included an illustration of the milk carton feeder, along with other examples of simple-to-assemble feeders you can make.

# Making a Bird Blind

S et up and decorate a bird blind for watching birds in your garden.

*Become a wildlife adventurer with a simple bird blind.*

## HERE'S WHAT YOU'LL NEED:

- 1 old, light-colored bedsheet
- 3 (6-foot) stakes or a fence from which to hang the blind
- 2 (1-foot) stakes or a fence
- 12 clothespins
- Marker
- Paints
- Paintbrushes
- Scissors
- Birdseed
- Field guide to birds

## HERE'S WHAT YOU'LL DO:

1. Take a walk around your garden and look for a place where birds spend time. If you have bird feeders, locate the blind in viewing distance. If not, just look and listen for bird activity and note where they are.

2. If you have a fence, you can hang the bird blind from it. If not, spread your sheet out on the ground. Place one of the 6-foot stakes at each end of the sheet and the remaining 6-foot stake in the middle. Drive the stakes at least 1 foot into the ground, and tie the rope between all three, pulling each corner of the rope down to the ground. Stake the ends of the rope into the ground with the 1-foot stakes.

3. Use clothespins to hang your sheet from the fence or rope.

4. Stand with your kids on one side of the bird blind and mark the sheet at the height of their eyes.

5. Cut 2 eyeholes out at the places you marked for each person planning to use the bird blind.

6. Take a look at the surrounding area. What colors do you see? What plants or objects? Paint your bird blind to camouflage with the surrounding area. Then allow the paint to dry.

7. Fill your bird feeder or, if you do not have a bird feeder, sprinkle birdseed on the opposite side of the sheet.

8. Sneak up to your bird blind stealthily, and regularly, to see if you can spot a bird in action without scaring it away. If you see a bird, take a close look. Note the size, colors, type of beak and feet. Can you see what it is doing? Where it flies to and from? How it communicates?

9. Take a look in a field guide to birds to see if you can identify the birds you see, or make up your own name based on its physical characteristics. For a complete online bird resource, visit birds.cornell.edu/.

# Invite Bats into Your Garden with a Bat Box

**M**ake your garden a welcome stop for bats. They will entertain you with their acrobatics and reward you with their phenomenal insect-eating skills.

Getting bats to occupy your bat box is not guaranteed. A study by Bat Conservation International found that about 60 percent of bat houses were inhabited over a 2-year period. Before you build or buy a bat house, consider that your chances of occupancy are higher if you live within $1/4$ mile of a natural water source like a pond or stream; bats like interior roost temperatures to be between 80 and 100 degrees, which means you might have to choose a specific exterior color or move your box to find the ideal space. Higher occupancy rates were also found in areas that had diverse habitats.

Our instructions are adapted from Bat Conservation International. This project involves light carpentry and is a great one for involving older children.

## HERE'S WHAT YOU'LL NEED:

1 sheet of $1/2$-inch CDX (outdoor grade) plywood, cut into a 2 × 4-foot piece

1 pine (furring) strip, 1 × 2 inches ($3/4$ × 1 $3/4$-inch finished) × 8 feet

30 (1-inch) exterior grade screws

1 quart flat, water-based paint, exterior grade

1 pint water-based primer, exterior grade

1 pint water-based, dark-colored stain, exterior grade

1 tube paintable latex caulk

Board measuring 1 × 4 × 28 inches for roof (optional, but recommended)

### Recommended tools:

Table saw or skill saw

Power drill with Phillips head bit

Drill bit to create pilot holes for screws

Tape measure

Caulking gun

Paintbrush

Pencil

## HERE'S WHAT YOU'LL DO:

1. Measure and cut plywood into 3 pieces and label as follows:
   26 $1/2$ × 24 inches: *backboard*
   16 $1/2$ × 24 inches: *front top*
   5 × 24 inches: *front bottom*

2. Roughen inside of backboard by cutting horizontal grooves with a sharp object or skill saw. This will serve as a surface for bats to cling to inside the bat house.

3. Measure and cut the pine strip into 1 piece of 24 inches and 2 pieces of 20 $1/4$ inches each.

4. Screw backboard to pine stripping, caulking

4

first. Start with the 24-inch piece on top. Then add the two 20 ¼-inch pieces along the sides. This will make a roosting chamber ³/₄-inch deep (consider drilling pilot holes in pine stripping to reduce the chance of wood splitting).

5 Stain the inside of the backboard, front top, and front bottom. The dark interior color helps keep it dark and warm inside.

6 Screw the front top onto the pine stripping, caulking first. Then screw the front bottom piece to the stripping, leaving a ½-inch space as a vent between the top and bottom front pieces. Don't forget to use caulk.

7 Caulk the exterior joints for good measure.

8 Attach roof piece on top, flush with the outside of backboard.

9 Prime and then paint the exterior of the house with at least 2 coats.

Bat houses can be installed on a building or a pole. Mount the box facing east or south, at least 12 feet above the ground in a place where the roost gets at least 6 hours of direct sunlight. For more information on creating and installing bat homes, including suggested exterior colors to paint your box, visit the Bat Conservation International website, batcon.org/index.php/get-involved/install-a-bat-house.html.

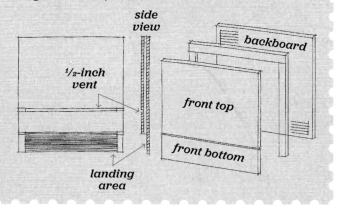

side view

½-inch vent

backboard

front top

front bottom

landing area

# ABOUT BATS

**BECAUSE OF HABITAT LOSS,** many bats are in search of new places to live, and you can make them a new home. Unfortunately, bats have a negative reputation, and many people associate them with vampires or rabies, or are afraid of how close they sometimes fly to our heads. But in reality, bats are a gardener's friend, and they are such deft flyers, there is really no chance they will come in contact with you. If they fly close, it is most likely because they are after the bugs that are attracted to you. If you don't handle a bat, there is no chance of acquiring rabies. Statistically, domestic dogs cause more harm to humans than these night flyers that account for 20 percent of all types of mammal species in the world! A colony of 150 big brown bats can eat 600,000 cucumber beetles per summer. And if that isn't enough of a reason to invite them into your yard, they also eat mosquitoes. As an added bonus, if your bat house is in a place where you can collect their scat, or guano, you will have a free, high--quality fertilizer.

4

## PROJECT

# Building a Barn Owl Box

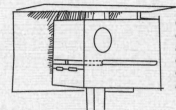

*Completed owl nest box with clean-out door on side and baffles*

A nesting family of barn owls can eat up to six rodents a night. That puts any house cat to shame. Barn owls are found throughout most of the world, and are uniquely accustomed to humans, which explains their tendency to roost in places like barns, buildings, and even a nest box that your family can make. Of course, you need an environment where barn owls live for your nest box to be occupied. Areas with open space like grasslands, farms, and open woodlands are where these winged creatures prey upon rats, gophers, voles, and other small mammals.

This design is adapted from the Lodi District Grape Growers Association, whose members encourage barn owls for pest control. This project involves light carpentry and is a great one for involving older children.

## HERE'S WHAT YOU'LL NEED:

1 sheet (8 × 4-foot) $\frac{1}{2}$-inch, 5-ply CDX (exterior grade) plywood

1 (16-foot) 4 × 4-inch post (or a structure to mount box 12 feet high)

1 (1-inch) dowel, 4 feet long

4 (1-inch) L brackets with $\frac{1}{2}$-inch screws

2 hex head bolts $\frac{1}{2}$ × 4 $\frac{1}{2}$ inches, with nuts and washers

4 carriage bolts, $\frac{1}{4}$ × 3 $\frac{1}{2}$ inches, with nuts and washers

2 (2-inch) hinges with screws

2 (13-inch) 2 × 2-inch lumber pieces for spacers

1 (1-inch) hook and eye for clean-out door

2 quarts of white paint, exterior grade

40 box nails, 1 $\frac{3}{4}$ inches

Wood glue

**Recommended tools:**

Table saw or skill saw

Power drill with Phillips head bit

$\frac{1}{2}$-inch and $\frac{1}{4}$-inch drill bits

1-inch hole saw bit

Hammer

Clamps

Hand jigsaw or keyhole saw

Posthole digger

Tape measure

Paintbrush or roller

Pencil

Barn owls are found all over the world. Invite one to your yard with a barn owl nest box.

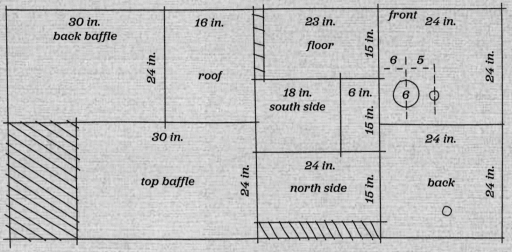

*Make an owl nest box from 1 sheet of ½-inch CDX plywood*

## HERE'S WHAT YOU'LL DO:

1. Paint both sides of plywood.

2. Cut all pieces from plywood per the diagram. Label all pieces.

3. Cut entrance hole, then drill 1-inch hole for dowel with front and back clamped together.

4. Using nails and wood glue, assemble the sides, floor, front, and back as shown in diagram. Attach hinged clean-out door last.

5. Using the 13-inch long 2 × 2s, center top baffle on roof panel and fasten baffle and roof to the 2 × 2s with ¼-inch carriage bolts.

6. Position four L brackets on the underside of the roof panel so that two will fit over each side

of the box during final assembly.

7. Drill and bolt the box, post, and back baffle together using ½-inch hex head bolts. The top of the post should be flush with the top of the box, while the back baffle should extend above it by 2 inches to align with the top baffle.

8. Attach the roof assembly to the box through the L brackets.

9. Insert dowel through the holes and glue it in place.

10. Erect the post with the box opening facing away from prevailing winds and storms.

Barn owl boxes should be mounted above 12 feet and ideally away from human activity. They can be mounted on buildings or trees instead of a post, but take care to protect from predators such as raccoons, squirrels, and snakes.

## Making a Pond or Bog for Wild Things

Water is an essential element for creating habitat for backyard wildlife. Water features can be elaborate, like a full pond with an electric-pumped waterfall, or simple, as in a tub or plastic-lined wine barrel filled with water, plants, and rocks. Water features are often available at garden centers, but you and your kids can also make your own. Whatever type of pond you choose, you can place halfway-submerged rocks and make shallow areas to turn your pond into a bath and lounge for birds. Adding perches or woody perennials near your pond will also serve as a welcome mat for your feathered friends.

Ponds can be a drowning hazard for toddlers and babies, and small children should never be left unsupervised near water features. If you have a baby and want a pond, you might consider putting a temporary fence around your pond, or just maintaining careful vigilance of your child until they are big enough to be safe around the pond. As an additional precaution, you can install a piece of plexiglass or metal grate cut to the dimensions of a small container pond, and submerge it a few inches below the surface of the water.

Here are a few water features common in family gardens, organized from simple to complex.

### Pond in a Planter

This is a small tub pond with planted edges. Build this little tub pond where you want it to be, since it will be quite heavy when you are done creating it. Use two plastic or galvanized steel tubs, one slightly smaller than the other. Put the smaller tub inside the larger tub and place rocks or bricks below the smaller tub, if needed, so that the lips of the tubs are at an even height. Together with your kids, fill the space in between the tubs with rocks on the bottom and then soil on the top layer. Plant low-growing plants, such as mounding thyme or trailing succulents like sedums in the soil that surrounds the inner tub. Now you and your kids can fill the inner tub with water and, if it is large enough, add a water plant or a rock for birds to land on.

## Creating a Pond from a Pre-formed Pond Liner

These plastic pools come in various shapes and sizes and are usually set in the ground with a rock and plant edging installed. It is ideal to add a fountain or mini waterfall, both of which require a small electric pump. John created a small stream that flows into his pre-formed pond with a piece of flexible pond liner and some rocks. Circulating the water makes a nice sound, oxygenates the water, and helps to agitate the water to discourage mosquito development. Small fountain and waterfall pumps can be found at home supply stores and most cost less than $100 dollars. These can be wired or solar powered. Solar pumps are often easier solutions because you don't need an electrical outlet nearby. Older kids make great water engineers and can help design and troubleshoot homemade waterfalls or streams. Directions on how to install a pre-formed pond liner can be found at pondsolutions.com/install-preformed-pond.htm.

## Creating a Pond from a Pond Kit

To make a more substantial water feature, ponds can be created with more elaborate kits, which include filtered waterfall boxes, skimmer boxes, and larger pumps. These are usually designed with a thick rubber pond liner that is laid over a dug-out area. By digging your own pond you can make areas of different depths and steps for plants, rocks, and bogs. There is much more flexibility in designing a pond with a rubber pond liner than with a pre-formed liner, but it does take more work and planning. Detailed instructions and videos on installing a flexible pond liner kit can be found online at pondliner.com/product/garden_pond_installation.

A team of teens built this pond; adding a gravel bottom is one of the final steps.

Water features take time to care for. If your pond gets too hot, algae will start to grow. It is unsightly and often clogs pumps. Creating a pond environment that includes plants to cover and shade the pond will help. Making the pond deep will also help to keep the water cool.

Adding other types of fish to ponds is quite fun, but often they can attract predators, like raccoons. Creating a hiding place for your fish, such as spaces between submerged rocks, can help.

Also try making a muddy area around your pond, and checking in the morning for tracks from nighttime visiting animals. You will be surprised by the number of critters that use your pond, from raccoons to snakes and great blue herons.

## Pets and Your Garden

"Mi casa es tu casa," or "My house is your house." We often extend this invitation to pets in our homes, but with boundaries that must be taught

*Sorry, pooch, this veggie patch isn't for you. • Stopping for a bit of refreshment during a long day of napping and playing.*

to our furry friends. The same is true with domesticated critters in our gardens. We need to set boundaries by either teaching them or setting up physical barriers, such as fences.

## Dogs

They may be man's best friend, but dogs can feel like your worst enemy if they dig up your garden. With proper planning and discipline, however, dogs can easily co-exist in the garden. Low livestock fencing is what we most commonly see erected as a barrier between a vegetable garden and an area for dogs to run, play, and nap. Other dogs we met were experts at staying on the paths in the garden, and some had even been trained to do their business in a particular spot in the yard. By involving your kids in training, and reminding your dogs about staying on pathways, you will also help reinforce this concept for your kids. Whatever your approach, it is important to keep your dog's feces and urine out of your

vegetable garden area and compost.

Dog houses and dog beds are a nice addition to a yard, and at times dogs help protect yards from visiting squirrels, cats, and other pests.

## Cats

Like dogs, cats can help protect your garden. Sly by nature, many are skillful at catching rodent pests. But their slyness also accounts for an uncanny ability to go where they are not welcome, such as a newly seeded garden bed. Worse, they often use garden beds as litter boxes. There are many products, such as scents, water guns, and noisemakers that work (to limited degrees) to keep these quick, light-footed creatures at bay. Covering a seedbed with a piece of chicken wire, floating row cover, newspaper, or even crisscrossed sticks can offer protection. Installing a cage or netting, however, is usually the most effective way to fully exclude cats from your garden beds.

*To kids, it doesn't matter which came first.*

There are a few plants that cats enjoy visiting in the garden. Catnip brings joy to many, and young grasses such as wheat, barley, oat, and rye are happily digested as supplemental roughage. By covering your vegetable beds and then planting these cat attractions around the garden, you can work to redirect feline visitors.

Not all plants in a garden are good for your pets. The American Society for the Prevention of Cruelty to Animals has an online database of over 400 plants that are toxic to dogs, cats, and horses. Learn more at aspca.org.

## Chickens

Kids love everything about chickens. Chickens are much easier to care for than most people think, and the benefits of having a garden flock are numerous. Besides being cute family pets and great kitchen scrap decomposers, they can also provide fresh eggs and meat as well as high-nitrogen manure. Before venturing down the path of creating a coop for your hens, check your city's regulations and talk to your neighbors to make sure that having a flock will not cause any major concerns. Of course, if you live in the city or have neighbors nearby, adding a rooster or even a boisterous flock of hens to your yard might be noisy enough to ruffle some feathers. Hens lay eggs just fine without a rooster, so you might want to skip the cock-a-doodle. You can expect around 250 eggs per year, per hen, for the first two or three years of the bird's life. Laying frequency varies by breed, so if you are looking for egg production make sure your chickens are a good laying breed, such as Rhode Island Reds. If you want

*Weed and fertilize at the same time with this movable chicken tractor.*

an exotic-looking flock, know that they might not produce as many eggs.

A coop consists of a run and a henhouse. A run is an enclosed area where your hens can roam around. It should be sunny and dry, as they like to take dust baths. The henhouse is the place where they sleep, and it includes a perch and nest boxes. The henhouse should be ventilated, with limited exposure to the outside elements. Coops should provide about 3 to 4 square feet per bird, and henhouses should be 1 to 2 square feet per bird. There are unlimited types of designs available in books and online, and with the increased popularity of backyard hens, we have even come across professional home henhouse builders. Ask around in your community and you may be surprised by the support you will find.

## FEATURES OF WELL-DESIGNED, FAMILY-FRIENDLY COOPS

- With the time demands of running a family, it is nice to be able to leave behind the worry of whether or not the hens are locked up. If you desire the pastoral appeal of having free-range chickens, know you can always let them out, but plan for a predator-proof coop for peace of mind. To make your coop fully predator-proof, we recommend that you include a totally enclosed run. Poultry wire works well for this. Bury poultry wire at least 12 inches deep and have it angle out (away from the coop) underground at least 6 inches to deter burrowing predators.

- Have nest boxes easily accessed from the outside of the coop, making it easy to collect eggs, and for your family and neighbors to easily check out the hens. You might also want to create a design that allows easy viewing of the inside of the henhouse. When Neli has buddies sleep over, before bedtime they love viewing and petting the perched, sleeping hens.

- Design your henhouse or coop with a place to keep the feed container dry during a rainstorm. You might also want a design that includes storage for items like straw for nest box bedding or bags of feed.

- Install an auto-watering dish. Fairly inexpensive and easily connected to a garden hose or faucet, this simple piece of barnyard technology makes sure your hens are hydrated when you are busy with other daily deeds.

- Make a henhouse that is easy to clean. John's henhouse has a door on the bottom. The bottom is raised a couple of feet off the ground and is made of half-inch hardware cloth padded with straw. This allows for ventilation and lets compostables fall through to the ground. These can then be easily transferred to the adjacent compost pile.

- Design for multiple purposes. We have seen henhouses that were the bottom layer of a kid's playhouse, saving space and keeping the hens in the center of attention. Make your hens your composters by building an easy-access door to dump your kitchen scraps next to the hen house. Hens are great at weeding, so think about ways to have your hens access your garden beds from the end of the season right up until spring planting. This can be done with chicken tractors, which are essentially mobile coops that can be moved to different parts of your yard. Movable fencing, such as plastic poultry wire, can also keep hens where you want them, and away from vulnerable areas, such as beds with baby plants.

Tamarah takes a break from exploring, playing, and hiding to go for a swing.

# Chapter 5

# GARDEN ADVENTURES AND Games

**SNEAK PEEK:** Let's go on a scavenger hunt •
Becoming human cameras • Creating magic spots •
Playing chickadees and jays • and more

*Family gardening is often a balance of play and work.*

In our kids' daily lives, they can easily forget that they are part of the natural world. They go to cupboards, grocery stores, school cafeterias, and restaurants for food; they go to faucets or bottles for water; they turn up a gas heater if they get cold; and they may even turn on the television if they want to watch wild animals in action.

An outdoor garden, however large or small, provides us with a phenomenal opportunity to help our kids grasp how all of us are, in fact, completely dependent upon the earth's natural resources for our survival. A child with a garden has a context for understanding that grains, fruits, and vegetables come from plants, and that plants don't grow without sun, soil, water, and air. As they spend more time in the garden and witness the vast array of ecological interactions taking place there, they are likely to see how animals provide us not only with meat, eggs, and milk, but also with many of the things we need to grow plants: fertile soil, in the case of a worm; protection from pests, in the case of a hawk or a wasp; and pollination for crops, in the case of a bee or hummingbird. In this sense, the family garden is an ideal setting for helping all of us bridge the vast divide that sometimes exists between our children (and ourselves) and the natural world around us.

When we plan Life Lab camps and field trips, we always make sure to balance gardening, harvesting, and cooking activities with some open-ended time for kids to engage all of their senses in garden adventures. Kids are natural explorers, and they are never more delighted than when they discover something new: a fly inside a carnivorous plant, a layer of fuzz on the edge of a leaf, a salamander under a board, or a cat track in the mud. These discoveries are teachable moments—while you are engaged in a garden task or even just a walk out to the car, welcome such interruptions and take time to appreciate their discoveries together. The activities here are all designed to help you engage your kids in sensory explorations of the garden. Whether they are searching for prickly plants or listening for birdcalls, you are certain to see your kids' enthusiasm and interest in the garden awaken as they begin to engage all of their senses.

PROJECT

# Let's Go on a Scavenger Hunt

Send your kids out on a scavenger hunt of the garden and see what they can find. This can be a fun team activity for groups of kids.

**HERE'S WHAT YOU'LL NEED:**

Cards or sheets with scavenger hunt list for each team

Pens or pencils for each team

**HERE'S WHAT YOU'LL DO:**

1. Tell your kids that the garden is full of all sorts of exciting things. By looking very carefully, they might find something they've never seen before.

2. Divide kids into two teams, and give each team a scavenger hunt list.

3. Have the teams go out and find all of the items on their list. The first team to return with all of their items wins the scavenger hunt (you might make a garden prize, like a strawberry smoothie or a packet of seeds, but you don't need a prize to motivate kids in this fun challenge).

5

CONTINUED →

Copy these scavenger hunt cards and send your kids exploring. Or make lists of your own.

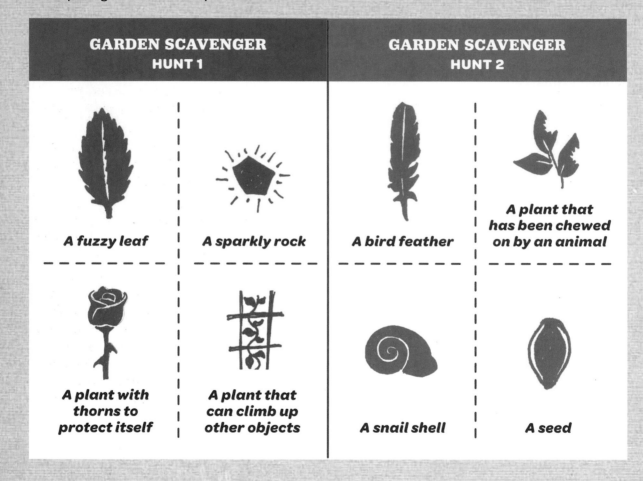

| GARDEN SCAVENGER HUNT 1 | | GARDEN SCAVENGER HUNT 2 | |
|---|---|---|---|
| A fuzzy leaf | A sparkly rock | A bird feather | A plant that has been chewed on by an animal |
| A plant with thorns to protect itself | A plant that can climb up other objects | A snail shell | A seed |

**ALSO TRY THIS:**

Have your kids observe the garden and then make their own scavenger hunt lists. Another take on this activity is to make treasure hunt lists that lead them from one clue to another. For example, "Find a place where worms and critters eat and poop all day long." At the compost pile you can have another clue leading them to the next spot.

# Blindfolded Meander

B lindfold a child and guide him or her through the garden, allowing them to take it in through their other senses.

**HERE'S WHAT YOU'LL NEED:**

Blindfold for each child

**HERE'S WHAT YOU'LL DO:**

1. Find a place in the garden that is full of great sensory experiences. We like to take our kids blindfolded through the sensory garden, where they can feel fuzzy flowers, smell geranium leaves, and hear the burbling of the fountain.

2. Talk to your kids about being blindfolded, and show them how you will be guiding them and keeping them safe. The safest way we have found to guide a blindfolded child is to walk slowly while holding her hand and elbow from the same side in both of your hands. To guide two or more children, have each child put their hands on the shoulders of the person in front of them.

3. If you are doing this with two or more children, get them in formation and then blindfold all of them.

4. Start guiding the front child slowly through the garden. Stop periodically to have them smell and feel things. You can pick objects and hand them to the children to pass back, or describe how they can reach out and touch things as they walk by.

5. Listen for birds singing, bees buzzing, and other interesting noises, and stop periodically to have them listen to the sounds of the garden.

6. Stop and pick a mint leaf, cherry tomato, raspberry, or other raw eating treat. Hand one to each child, have him or her take a taste and then guess what it is.

7. Plan your blindfold walk so that you end up in a beautiful place when they remove their blindfolds. We sometimes walk kids under the kiwi arbor, and then have them tilt their heads up towards the sky before removing their blindfolds. They are always awe-struck when they finally open their eyes and see a dense green kiwi jungle with fuzzy brown fruit above.

5

# *Solo Garden Ramble*

*Make garden exploration cards for your kids; soon they will be making their own.*

K ids very rarely have a chance to be outdoors alone. It can create a very magical feeling. In this activity, you will set up a trail of notes to your child, and then stand back while your child follows the trail through the garden.

## HERE'S WHAT YOU'LL NEED:

- Index cards
- Colored pens or pencils

## HERE'S WHAT YOU'LL DO:

1. Find a trail through a garden that has lots of variety and interesting plants or other things to look at.
2. Walk the trail alone, and stop every few feet to write a note to your child, encouraging them to use one of their senses to experience the world around them. It might say, "Hey, did you hear that? Stop here and listen until you hear three different bird sounds." Or, "Mmmm. What is that smell? Pick a leaf of this plant and smell it. What does it remind you of?"
3. Draw arrows onto cards and place them on the trail if there is an area where they might turn off of the path.
4. Show your child the beginning of the trail of notes, and leave them to follow it through the garden. Of course, you will be supervising them, but do so subtly, allowing them to feel like they are out there on their own.

## ALSO TRY THIS:

Have your kids make trails with notes for you or for their friends. If they are pre-literate, you can help them write and draw each card.

# Observing Square-Foot Habitats

Searching for the 100 million microbes in a handful of soil.

Y ou and your kids will see the world through the eyes of a tiny creature as you take some time to explore a garden micro-habitat together.

## HERE'S WHAT YOU'LL NEED:

4 rulers or 4 pieces of string, each cut
  1 foot long
Drawing paper
Pencils

## HERE'S WHAT YOU'LL DO:

1 Help your child find a small area of the garden that calls out to them.

2 Have them make a square by placing the 4 rulers or pieces of string at right angles to one another.

3 Lie down on your bellies with your face right at the edge of the square and shrink down in your imaginations. Look at that square foot as if it were your whole home. Where would you go to find shelter in the rain? Where would you go for water? What would you do for fun? Have your kids look for anything their imaginations come up with: slides, ladders, pools, mountains, you name it.

4 If they want to, your kids can draw maps of their little habitats. They can name the features or embellish their maps however they like.

## ALSO TRY THIS:

Your kids may want to change their square-foot habitat. Maybe they want to bring in a little twig bench for the insects to rest on, create an umbrella with a dry leaf to make a shelter from the rain, or build a teeter-totter out of sticks. Give them time and encouragement to make that little spot their own. Consider having your kids leave their micro-habitat marked for a couple of days, returning daily to observe changes.

5

Gardens are a great place to check things out.

5

# Creating Magic Spots

There is no greater way for a child or an adult to establish a connection with a piece of land than by sitting in a single spot for a few minutes each day, week after week, season after season, observing the natural goings-on in that place.

**HERE'S WHAT YOU'LL DO:**

1. Help your kids find a magic spot, a special place in the garden to call their own. They are much more likely to do this if you have your own magic spot to visit at the same time.

2. Explain that wild creatures (from robins to earthworms) are shy, and they will only come out if we get perfectly still and they are able to forget we are there. Make your spots comfortable by clearing a sitting area or placing a stump to lean back on.

3. Take a few minutes every day, or as often as possible, to head out to your magic spots. If you want, bring a journal or camera to record observations. Sit quietly, tuning into each of your senses. How many sounds can you hear? How does the wind feel on your cheeks? What smells are traveling in the air? What do you see in the area around you?

4. After each visit, share any exciting discoveries or thoughts you had with one another. After sitting alone for even a few minutes in an outdoor setting, kids will often return with heaps of stories about strange sounds they heard, bugs that crawled on their shoes, or pretty flowers they found that weren't there just a few days before.

# Becoming Human Cameras

*(Adapted from Joseph Cornell's Sharing Nature with Children II)*

*The garden is full of breathtaking views, both large and small.*

**B**y pretending to be cameras and photographers, you and your kids will start to see the garden in a whole new light.

## HERE'S WHAT YOU'LL DO:

1. Show your child how you will guide her safely, and then have her close her eyes. Tell her, "Now I'm the photographer, and you're the camera."

2. Walk slowly, holding her hand and elbow in your own hands, until you arrive at a nice viewing point. You might be looking at a big sweeping vista of the surrounding area, or you might bring her face right up close to a sunflower petal catching the sunlight.

3. Now tell your human camera to open her eyes when you tug gently on her earlobe.

4. Tug gently to have her take a picture and then close her eyes again.

5. Do this a few times, taking pictures of various garden delights. Then offer to trade positions and let your budding photographer guide you around the garden.

## ALSO TRY THIS:

After being a human camera, your child may enjoy taking actual photos of the garden. Print up the nice shots for a garden gallery, a note card for a grandparent, or to use in a scavenger hunt, returning to try and find the exact spot in the garden.

# Playing Chickadees and Jays

This is a great game for a group of kids. Each child will pretend to be a small bird with a nest and some baby birds to feed. Their job is to get food to their baby birds without letting the jays see where their nest is.

## HERE'S WHAT YOU'LL NEED:

1 small cup per child

A bowlful of dry beans

## HERE'S WHAT YOU'LL DO:

1. Talk with your kids about chickadees and jays. Explain that chickadees are little birds that build nests in trees. Jays are larger birds and they are nest robbers. This means that jays will eat eggs right out of the nest if they can. Ask your kids, "How do you think the chickadees protect their baby birds?" Talk about camouflaging their nests, flying quietly, misleading the jays by flying to various locations, and other strategies the chickadees might use.

2. Now it's time to pretend to be chickadees and jays. Ask for one or two children to be jays. The rest will be chickadees.

3. Place a bowlful of dry beans in a central location in the garden. Tell your kids, this is the food for the baby chickadees. The babies can't fly yet, so as the parent birds, they'll have to deliver the food to their nests.

4. Give each chickadee a cup, which represents their nest. Have the jays close their eyes and give the chickadees a minute to hide their nests in the garden.

5. When the chickadees return, it's time to play. Station yourself near the food source, and explain that chickadees can take 1 bean at a time. Their goal is to collect as many beans as possible in their nest cups. If a jay finds a nest, he can take all the beans for himself and throw the nest on the ground. Then the chickadee's job is to re-hide the nest and start over with collecting food, all without being spotted by the jay.

6. Play for a few minutes and then call everyone together to see who collected the most food for their babies. Talk about strategies used by both the chickadees and the jays and then rotate roles and play again.

## ALSO TRY THIS:

If you have a big enough space, play Human Camouflage. Instead of hiding nests, have the kids hide themselves. This is like hide-and-seek, but in this version the seeker can't move and the hiders must camouflage themselves and hide in a line of sight of the seeker. The last person spotted by the seeker becomes the new seeker.

Be your own
mason by making
hypertufa pots
and figures.

# Chapter 6

ART *in the Garden:* FUN Projects FOR ALL

- - - - - - - - - - - - - - - - - - - - - - - - - -

**SNEAK PEEK: Making flower dolls • Muddy miniature masterpieces • Hypertufa flower pots • Mosaic stepping stones • and more**

**T**hrough the centuries, artists from Botticelli to Monet have found inspiration in gardens. A bountiful garden is full of colors, textures, and shadows that will tantalize your senses and elicit creative expression. Amazingly, your garden can also provide many of the raw materials for making beautiful art. By using rocks for plant markers, gourds for birdhouses, and your imagination for inspiration, you and your kids can harvest much more than food from your garden.

At Life Lab, we have a garden art workshop just prior to the holidays. Parents and children come together to make flower-stamped wrapping paper, lavender dream pillows, and other gifts for those they love. We all find it deeply satisfying to make beautiful objects together in the garden. And at the end of the day, we have a handful of delightful, thoughtful gifts ready well ahead of schedule.

*Painted gourd bird feeders hang out to dry.*

# Gourd Maracas, Pets, and Birdhouses

Y ou and your kids can use the hard shells of gourds, along with a big dose of imagination, to create birdhouses, maracas, pets, and more.

## HERE'S WHAT YOU'LL NEED:

Gourds

Newspaper

Scissors

Rubbing alcohol

Sand paper

Decorating supplies, such as markers or paint, glue, googly eyes, string, feathers, and tissue paper

A dust mask

A drill with a $3/8$-inch bit and a hole-drilling attachment for your desired hole diameter (1 inch, $1^1/8$ inches, $1^1/4$ inches, $1^1/2$ inches, or 2 inches)

### For bean-filled maracas only:

Beans

Tape or a hard wax plug

### For birdhouse only:

Polyurethane sealer

Wire or twine for hanging birdhouse

## HERE'S WHAT YOU'LL DO:

1. If the weather permits, leave your gourds in the garden on the vine until they are dry. You can also dry them off the vine. When drying them off the vine, gently wash your gourds with soap and warm water to remove dirt, and then wipe them down with rubbing alcohol to kill any bacteria. Place the gourds on newspaper in a warm, dry, well-ventilated area to dry. Make sure they are not touching one another. Turn the gourds regularly and remove any that start to form soft spots.

2. Mold may occur on the outside of the gourd during the drying process. This is normal. You can sand it off once the gourd is fully dry.

3. You'll know your gourds are fully dried when you pick them up and shake them and the seeds rattle around inside. This may take up to 6 weeks.

4. Once you have a dried gourd, you can use your decorating supplies to make it into a maraca, a gourd pet, or a birdhouse.

5. For a maraca, or a musical shaker, simply decorate the outside of the gourd. Hold it by the narrow neck and shake it to make music. You can also put on a dust mask, drill a hole, remove the seeds, and replace them with dry beans or grains. Then patch the hole with tape or a hard wax plug for a different sound.

6. For a gourd pet, decorate the gourd to look like an animal. You might make a swan, a pig,

CONTINUED →

*It's a bird, it's a plane–it's a whale gourd.*

**6**

a whale, or a mythological creature. Your imagination is the only limit to what animal your gourd might become. Make a bunch of them to create a gourd jungle or zoo.

7 For a gourd birdhouse, put on a dust mask and drill a hole just above the center of the round part of the gourd. Use a knife and spoon to break up the innards and clean out the inside. Then drill 5 holes of $3/8$ inch each in the bottom of the gourd for drainage and ventilation, and 2 holes the same size on the top to put wire or rope through. Finally, seal the entire exterior with a polyurethane sealer. Hang your

birdhouse in the garden, at least 6 feet off the ground, and watch to see if a bird family decides to make it a home.

**Note:** Different birds will enter different sized holes. A chickadee, for example, will prefer a $1 1/8$-inch hole, while a bluebird will prefer a hole that's at least $1 1/2$ inches wide. To make a birdhouse for a specific kind of bird in your region, you can research the appropriate birdhouse entrance hole diameter at birds.cornell.edu. Alternately, you can just make a hole and see who comes to visit or stay awhile.

# *Making a Garden Journal*

You and your kids can use sticks, flowers, and leaves from the garden to make and decorate garden journals for keeping track of seeds sown, birdcalls heard, weather patterns, and more.

## HERE'S WHAT YOU'LL NEED:

- 3 sheets of 8½ × 11-inch watercolor paper
- A rubber band
- A hole punch
- Colored pencils or crayons

## HERE'S WHAT YOU'LL DO:

1. Cut your paper into quarters.

2. Stack your 12 quarter-papers and punch 2 holes along the left side, one that is 1 inch from the top and another, 1 inch from the bottom.

3. Take a walk and find a pretty 4-inch stick. You can always cut a longer stick to make it 4 inches.

4. Wrap the rubber band over one end of the stick, then pass it through the top hole of the paper. Now stretch the rubber band to the bottom hole and pass it back up and through, wrapping it around the bottom end of your stick. Congratulations! You have made a garden journal.

5. Make a cover for your journal using colored pencils or crayons. Give it a title, such as "Jasmine's Garden Journal." Then decorate it with a picture of your garden, your favorite plant, or whatever else you choose.

6. Use your journal to record garden plans, ideas, and memories, like what you want to plant next spring, a picture of a bird you saw in the garden, the names of your favorite flowers, or a recipe for making pesto with basil.

# Making Dolls from Flowers

*Flower dolls in all their finery.*

**G**ather flowers with your kids and use them to make miniature fairies, farmers, animals, or anything else that comes to mind.

**HERE'S WHAT YOU'LL NEED:**

Toothpicks
Scissors or hand shears

**HERE'S WHAT YOU'LL DO:**

1. Take a walk around the garden together and look for flowers and flower parts to use for your dolls. A large petal might make a nice skirt. The stamen in the center of the flower might do for arms and legs. The sky is the limit on this.

2. Harvest your flowers and flower parts.

3. Use vines or long grasses to tie your flower pieces together and create flower dolls.

**ALSO TRY THIS:**

You can make fruit or vegetable dolls. Chives make great hair, beets can be used as faces, and celery can serve as arms and legs. Again, the possibilities are endless, so let your imagination run wild.

You can also make a simple flower doll from a flower that is ideally suited for doll-making. Snapdragons, for example, make great little faces with mouths that open and close. You can also make a hollyhock doll in just seconds. Simply pick a flower and use a paper clip or toothpick to poke a hole in the center. Turn it upside down to make the skirt. Now pick an unopened flower bud with some stem attached. Push the stem through the hole in the flower and you have a hollyhock doll.

# *Creating Fairy Houses and Critter Condos*

*Tea time for fairy and duckie.*

**Y**ou and your kids can let your imaginations run wild as you use natural building materials to make miniature homes for garden fairies or critters.

## HERE'S WHAT YOU'LL NEED:

Natural building materials, such as twigs, bark, moss, stones, leaves, and other garden treasures

String

Glue

Miniature fairy figures to place in and around the homes (optional)

## HERE'S WHAT YOU'LL DO:

1. Building fairy homes is a brilliantly simple activity. First, collect building materials from your garden. Twigs make great beams; moss makes a lovely, plush carpet; bark can be used for walls; stones for walkways; and dry leaves for roof tiles.

2. Design a home for a fairy. If you like, you can create a sign in front of the home welcoming garden fairies or other creatures passing through.

3. If you are making a more permanent fairy home, in a container for example, you can select succulents, ferns, groundcover, or other plants with small leaves and flowers to grow around the house. Visit miniature-gardening. com for a list of plants that can be used to represent trees, shrubs, groundcover, and flower beds in your tiny world. You can also find fairies, bridges, small garden tools, and more here.

## ALSO TRY THIS:

You may want to invite friends over and work together to create a fairy village. We have seen fairy farms, markets, parks, and flyways. Let your imagination guide you and just see what emerges. You can also use flowers to make fairies to inhabit these homes.

6

# Muddy Miniature Masterpieces

Add water and
my whiskers
might grow.

**U**se your bare feet to mix up a batch of mud, and then build sculptures with your kids and dry them in the sun. This is a great activity for a large group.

## HERE'S WHAT YOU'LL NEED:

2 tarps that you don't mind getting dirty

1 bucket of water

1 hose

A big pile of clay-like soil

A large compost sifter or a small-holed nursery tray

Pieces of cardboard cut into 1-foot squares; one for each sculpture

## HERE'S WHAT YOU'LL DO:

1. Gather a pile of clay-like soil, with at least 3 heaping handfuls for each child. If your native soil is sandy rather than clay-like, you can add powdered clay purchased at a construction supply or art store.

2. Sift the soil over a tarp, breaking up or removing all clods.

3. Mound the sifted soil on the tarp and press a crater into the top of the mound.

4. Fill the crater with water and mix up the mud by walking on it with bare feet. Continue to add water until your mud has the consistency of wet pottery clay or Play Dough. If it gets too wet, add more soil.

5. When your mud is ready, have your kids clean their feet by dipping them in bucket(s) filled with water on the second tarp.

6. Now have each child pick up a large handful of mud and make a sculpture. They might build an animal, a house, a pinch pot, or anything else they can think of.

7. Place each sculpture on a piece of cardboard and set it in the sun to dry.

6

┌ PROJECT ┐

# The Fine Art of Flower Pounding

*Pounded flower bookmarks make great gifts.*

**W**hat kid doesn't love hitting things with a hammer? In this activity, you will harvest flowers together and then pound them onto paper, leaving a beautiful flower print behind.

## HERE'S WHAT YOU'LL NEED:

- Cutting board
- Dishtowel
- Fresh flowers and leaves
- Hammers
- Wide painter's tape
- Watercolor paper cut into bookmarks or note cards

## ALSO TRY THIS:

You can do this same thing with fabric. Simply place the fabric over upright flowers and pound directly on it until you see the color of the flower coming through the cloth.

## HERE'S WHAT YOU'LL DO:

1. Place a cutting board on top of a dishtowel. Place a piece of watercolor paper on top of the cutting board.

2. Harvest a handful of fresh flowers and leaves. Note that some flowers work better for flower pounding than others, so harvest a variety to test out.

3. Cut the stems and as much of the green back off of the flowers as possible. If the flower has a large center, remove it and use only the petals.

4. Place the flowers and leaves face down on the watercolor paper. For large flowers, only place the petals on the paper.

5. To remove some of the tack from the painter's tape, stick it to your pant leg a time or two.

6. Now cover the flowers and leaves completely with a single layer of painter's tape.

7. Pound on the tape with a hammer, making sure to hit each section multiple times. You can place a phone book below the paper to dampen the noise.

8. Carefully peel off some of the tape and peek at the paper to see if any area needs more pounding.

9. When you're satisfied with the print, peel off all of the tape. The colors should have left a print on your paper.

10. Remove any flower or leaf pieces that are still stuck to the paper.

11. Now allow your paper to dry and use it for a note card, bookmark, or anything else you can think of. Laminating bookmarks makes for a nice finishing touch.

6

# Hypertufa Flower Pots

Together with your kids, you can create hypertufa planters which resemble the porous tufa stone found around the world. Kids can help with every step, from choosing molds—which could be bowls, nursery pots, or boxes—to making and planting in the pots. These pots are easy to make, and they are very durable and attractive, especially if left out over time to grow moss or lichen. They look especially good planted with succulents. This is also a great activity for large groups; simply make more hypertufa by multiplying the recipe.

## HERE'S WHAT YOU'LL NEED:

Tarp or newspapers

2 pot molds, 1 slightly larger than that other

Nonstick cooking spray

Face masks (to avoid breathing cement and perlite dust)

Gloves

Large tub or wheelbarrow to mix the ingredients

Large empty coffee can for measuring

1 coffee can of Portland cement

2 coffee cans of sieved coco peat (potting mix ingredient, purchased at nurseries)

1 coffee can of perlite (potting mix ingredient, purchased at nurseries)

1 coffee can of water

Sticks or small dowels

## HERE'S WHAT YOU'LL DO:

1. Cover your work surface with a tarp or newspapers.

2. Put on gloves and a mask and measure out 1 part cement, 2 parts coco peat, and 1 part perlite, using the coffee can. Mix the ingredients in a tub or wheelbarrow, using your gloved hands.

3. Thoroughly mix the water into the dry ingredients. It should have the texture of very thick oatmeal and should hold its shape and not drip water when squeezed.

4. Lightly spray the inside of the larger mold and the outside of the smaller mold with nonstick cooking spray.

5. Working from the bottom up, firmly pack a 1- to 1½-inch layer of the mixture into the bottom of the bigger (outer) mold.

6. If the small mold container does not have a hole in its bottom, make a few drainage holes. You will poke a stick or dowel through them to make drainage holes in the mixture.

7. Center the smaller (inner) mold inside of the bigger mold so that there is an equidistant space between the outer and inner mold.

8. Pack mixture into the space made between the outer and inner mold, filling it in well.

9. Insert a stick or dowel through the bottom of the inner mold to create a drainage hole in the mixture.

10. Lightly cover the pot with plastic and let it dry for a few days. Remove the molds, and plant.

# Mosaic Stepping Stones

This beautiful stepping stone is made from glass tiles.

A quick and easy way to make attractive stepping stones for your garden.

## HERE'S WHAT YOU'LL NEED:

Tarp or newsprint

Pie tin, disposable aluminum casserole, or other disposable tray-like container

Portland cement

Glass beads, shells, marbles, shards of ceramic dishes

Gloves

Bucket and mixing stick

Water

## HERE'S WHAT YOU'LL DO:

1. Cover your workspace with tarps or newsprint.
2. Mix up a batch of cement in a bucket per instructions.
3. Pour or scoop cement into trays at least 1 1/2 inches deep.
4. Gently shake tray to level cement.
5. Place decorative items in the cement so that they are stuck in the cement but still show on top. You might need to let the cement thicken up for 30 minutes or so to keep objects from sinking in the cement. Leave tray to dry overnight, and give your cement stone another couple of days before stepping on it.

## ALSO TRY THIS:

A more involved process to making stepping stones involves sticking mosaic pieces to a pre-purchased paver or stepping stone with thin-set mortar. After the mosaic pieces have dried, you add a layer of grout. This is much more involved than the steps listed above and takes more patience than many kids have, but the grout makes for a very professional look. Visit making-mosaics.com/mosaic-stepping-stones.html and mosaicartsupply.com to learn more about supplies and tips for making mosaics.

6

# No-Sew Potpourri Sachets

*Sachets are easy for small hands to fill.*

These fragrant, colorful sachets are great for freshening up drawers and closets. This no-sew version is easy for all ages to make, and it's a great way to use up fabric remnants.

## HERE'S WHAT YOU'LL NEED:

Fabric scraps cut into pieces that are 4 1/2 inches square

Fabric glue

Raffia, ribbon, or twine

1/3 cup potpourri mixture for each sachet

Label with the potpourri ingredients (optional)

*For the potpourri mixture, use any combination of fragrant dried plants such as allspice, bay leaves, calendula, cardamom pods, cedar, chamomile, cinnamon sticks, citrus peel, cloves, eucalyptus, lavender, lemon balm, lemon verbena, nutmeg, peppermint leaves, rose buds and petals, rosemary, or others.*

## HERE'S WHAT YOU'LL DO:

1. For each sachet, place 2 matching fabric squares together with the pattern facing out. Glue the edges together on 3 sides. Spread the glue close to the edges to prevent fraying. Dry several hours or overnight.

2. Create the potpourri mixture.

3. Once the glue is dry, fill each sachet with about 1/3 cup of potpourri mixture. Glue together the open edge and allow to dry.

4. Arrange the finished sachets in a stack and tie them together with raffia, ribbon, or twine.

5. Attach a label, if desired.

## ALSO TRY THIS:

You can purchase small mesh or cloth bags with drawstrings to make the project even easier. In this case, just fill the bags and tie off the strings. You can also make sachets in any shape. Together with your kids, choose a fabric you like and then come up with a fun shape, like a heart, for example. Then cut, sew, and fill the pillow as described above.

6

# Pressed Leaf or Flower Candles

These beautiful candles are simple to make, yet very impressive as gifts. Children of all ages can choose their favorite leaves or flowers and press them. Older kids can also help with preparing the flora and dipping the candles in the wax.

## HERE'S WHAT YOU'LL NEED:

Pillar candles, at least 2 inches wide

Pressed leaves or flowers

White glue or decoupage medium

Inexpensive artists' paintbrushes

6 cups paraffin wax, roughly chopped

Large cooking pot and water

Tin can large enough to fit the candles, such as a 28-ounce size

Pliers

Toothpick

Waxed paper

*Cooled, unused paraffin wax can be kept in the can and heated again to make additional candles.*

## HERE'S WHAT YOU'LL DO:

1. First you'll need to press some leaves or flowers. Walk around the garden and choose your favorites. Place each leaf or bloom between the pages of a heavy, hardbound book. Pile other heavy books on top of this one and leave for at least 2 weeks.

2. Once your leaves or flowers are ready, carefully paint glue or decoupage medium onto their backs. Place them onto the candles and allow them to dry. If some parts stick up, you will be able to press them down into the wax after you dip them.

3. Fill a pot halfway with water and place on medium heat. Put the chopped paraffin wax into the tin can, filling it two-thirds full. Place the can in the water and melt the wax, stirring occasionally. Remove the can from the pot once the wax is melted.

4. Using pliers, pick up a candle by the wick and dip it completely into the melted wax to seal the leaves or flowers onto the candle. Slowly pull the candle out and place it on waxed paper.

5. Press any lifting parts into the cooling wax with a toothpick. Dip the candle again if desired. Place on a piece of wax paper and allow candle to cool completely.

# Garden Snapshots

*These two shots were taken by second graders in a school garden.*

**HERE'S WHAT YOU'LL NEED:**

> Digital camera
>
> Blank note cards
>
> Double stick tape
>
> Raffia or ribbon
>
> Cellophane bags (optional)

**HERE'S WHAT YOU'LL DO:**

1. Start by showing your child how to carry and care for the camera, how to take and erase pictures, and how to change the camera settings for close-up shots.

2. Explore the garden together and take pictures.

3. Download and print your favorite photographs.

4. Tape the photos onto the front of the blank note cards. Stack several cards and envelopes together and tie with raffia or ribbon, or enclose cards and envelopes in cellophane bags and secure with raffia or ribbon.

It is such a joy to explore a garden through the lens of a camera. Children have a particularly wonderful time and take beautiful, unexpected photographs. There are also many simple digital photo applications for phones and cameras these days that can lend a professional, artistic flair to almost any photo. Assemble several cards in a bundle and you have a lovely, practical gift.

6

# Leaf Impression Stationery

*Practice makes perfect with leaf print and pressed leaf cards.*

Leaf prints are a great way to dress up stationery. You can also use this technique to decorate brown kraft gift bags or wrapping paper; leaf prints are even beautiful enough to frame.

**HERE'S WHAT YOU'LL NEED:**

Newspaper

Flexible, sturdy leaves

Acrylic paint in bowls or cups

Sponge brush

Paper towels, cut in half

Printing brayer (available at craft supply stores) or large spoon

Thick, white paper cut slightly smaller than the note cards

Blank note cards and envelopes

Double stick tape

Raffia or ribbon

**HERE'S WHAT YOU'LL DO:**

1. Take a walk around the garden and collect intact, flexible, sturdy leaves with unique shapes.

2. Cover a work area with newspaper.

3. Using the sponge brush, apply a thin coat of acrylic paint to the underside of a leaf.

4. Place the leaf, paint side down, onto the paper. Cover the leaf with a paper towel. Roll over the paper towel with a brayer or go over with the back of a spoon, pressing firmly.

5. Lift the paper towel and leaf. Repeat this process, each time using a new paper towel.

6. To change paint colors, rinse and dry the leaf.

7. Allow the leaf prints to dry.

8. Attach the leaf prints to the front of the cards with double stick tape. Stack into a bundle with envelopes and tie with raffia or ribbon.

6

# Birdseed Wreaths

Kids, adults, and birds alike love these festive wreaths. They are easy to make and create terrific gifts. They look wonderful hanging in trees or in windows. Makes 12 small wreaths.

*A winter feast for our feathered friends.*

## HERE'S WHAT YOU'LL NEED:

1 cup water

Measuring cup

3 cups wild birdseed

$1/2$ cup dried cranberries

$1/2$ cup raw nuts, roughly chopped

2 envelopes of gelatin

Raffia, ribbon, or twine

Waxed paper

Cellophane bags

## HERE'S WHAT YOU'LL DO:

1. Bring $3/4$ cup of water to a boil.

2. In a large bowl, sprinkle 2 envelopes of gelatin over $1/4$ cup of cold water. Let the mixture sit for 1 minute.

3. Add the hot water to the bowl and stir for 3 minutes, or until the gelatin has completely dissolved.

4. Add the birdseed, cranberries, and nuts and blend well. Let the mixture set for a few minutes, and then stir again. Repeat until the mixture is cool and workable.

5. Divide the mixture into 12 balls (or fewer for larger wreaths) and place on sheets of waxed paper.

6. Flatten the birdseed balls slightly, form holes in the centers and let dry overnight.

7. Loop raffia, ribbon, or twine through the center of the wreaths to hang.

8. Package in cellophane bags, tie with additional raffia, ribbon, or twine, and attach a label, if desired.

6

# Rock Plant Markers

*Rubber-stamped stones make great plant markers and gifts.*

**HERE'S WHAT YOU'LL NEED:**

Flat rocks

Acrylic enamel paints

Inexpensive artists' paintbrushes

**HERE'S WHAT YOU'LL DO:**

1. Collect some smooth flat rocks that are large enough to write across. Or purchase beach stones at a construction supply store.

2. Scrub your rocks clean and then set in the sun until completely dry.

3. Paint the name of a garden plant on each rock. If you like, you can also paint a picture of the plant.

4. Place your rock next to those plants in your garden.

**ALSO TRY THIS:**

Use rubber stamps with the letters of the alphabet to write words on your stones. To keep your stamps in alphabetical order when not in use, you can stick them into a floral arrangement foam block.

**H**elp your kids paint the names of your garden plants onto rocks. Then they can place these rocks as labels throughout the garden. These plant labels are free, lovely, and sure to stay put on a windy day.

*Preparing dinner, from garden to table.*

# Chapter 7

# Cooking From The Garden:
## Snacks, Meals, and Other Tasty Activities

- - - - - - - - - - - - - - - - - - - - - - - - - - - - - - - -

**SNEAK PEEK:** Cooking tasks for every age •
Harvest applesauce • Garden pizzas • Green garden
smoothies • Cooking with the sun • and more

*Harvesting ingredients for a delicious—and healthy—dinner.*

here is no getting around it: gardening is hard work. One thing that can keep you committed to your garden over the long haul is the innate joy you will find in reaping its many rewards. Whether you and your kids are pulling a carrot from the ground, drinking nectar from a sage flower, or having a community-wide tomato harvest party, make sure to find time to enjoy the fruits of your labor together—it will help keep your inspiration alive year after year.

Kids who are involved in harvesting and preparing healthy foods from the garden are also more likely to eat them. This is great news for the health-conscious parent. So if you wish your child would eat more vegetables, one of the best things you can do is grow, harvest, and prepare some vegetables together.

## Kitchen Tools for Kids

Using kid-sized kitchen implements will help keep your children safe and provide them with opportunities to be helpful and excited about food preparation. In the Life Lab Garden Classroom, we invite kids of all ages to use mortars and pestles, eggbeaters, measuring cups, salad spinners, blenders, hand-held juicers, apple corers, and more.

We also have knives for different age groups. The youngest children simply tear things apart with their hands. With very close supervision and careful instruction, once they are about 5 years old, we invite our young visitors to chop soft fruits and vegetables using nylon knives designed specifically for children, such as those sold by Curious Chef and Kuhn Rikon Kinderkitchen. In order to make chopping and slicing easier, we pre-steam hard vegetables, such as carrots and beets. For children 7 to 11 years old, we have round-tipped, serrated steak

*Snacks*

### Sunny Seed Green Bean Pâté

Even green bean fanatics can struggle to keep up with the harvest on a productive green bean patch. This unique spread gives green beans a new look and feel while preserving their wonderful taste. Older kids can help with every step, and kids of all ages can help prepare the green beans for cooking and blend the ingredients together.

ACTIVE TIME: *30 minutes*   TOTAL TIME: *30 minute*
*Makes about 3 cups*

**Here's what you'll need:**

> 2 large onions, peeled and thinly sliced
> 1 tablespoon olive oil
> 1 pound green beans, trimmed and
>     cut into ½-inch pieces
> 8 cups water
> 1 cup sunflower seeds, roasted
> 2 teaspoons salt
> 3 scallions, chopped
> Sliced bread or crackers (optional)
> Large frying pan
> Large pot
> Colander
> Food processor or blender

*Gathering ingredients for Sunny Seed Green Bean Pâté.*

**Here's what you'll do:**

1. Heat oil in a frying pan and sauté onion until soft and lightly browned.
2. In a large pot, bring the water to a boil. Add cut green beans and continue to boil for 4 to 5 minutes. Once tender, drain the green beans into a colander, reserving ½ cup of the cooking water for later use.
3. Grind the sunflower seeds in a food processor or blender. Add green beans, salt, chopped scallions and the reserved ½ cup of cooking water and continue to blend until creamy.
4. Serve pâté with bread or crackers.

## Zucchini Baba Ga–what?
## Baba Ganoush

Have you ever walked into your garden and found a zucchini the size of a baseball bat? Maybe you were on vacation when it grew, or maybe it was just hidden beneath some leaves. Either way, this recipe is wonderfully delicious, and also a great way to use ripe and even over-ripe zucchini. And by the way, it's pronounced "bah-bah gah-noosh."

ACTIVE TIME: *20 minutes*   TOTAL TIME: *45 minutes*
*Makes about 2 cups*

### Here's what you'll need:

*5 medium-sized zucchini (about 8 inches*
*in length), or the equivalent with smaller*
*or larger zucchinis*
*¼ cup plus 1 tablespoon olive oil,*
*divided and kept separate*
*¼ cup tahini*
*1 to 2 cloves garlic, chopped*
*6 tablespoons lemon juice*
*½ teaspoon salt (or more to taste)*
*2 tablespoons chives, chopped (optional)*
*Large baking sheet*
*Food processor or blender*

### Here's what you'll do:

❶ On a large baking sheet, roast the zucchini whole under the oven broiler until they are soft and the skins start to blacken, about 3–5 minutes per side. Turn them periodically so all sides become charred. Remove the baking

*Greta prefers her zucchini raw.*

sheet from the oven and set aside to cool. Once the zucchini are cool enough to handle, cut them in half lengthwise and scrape the insides into a bowl. Discard the charred rind.

❷ In a food processor or blender, add the zucchini insides, ¼ cup olive oil, tahini, chopped garlic, lemon juice and salt. Blend until smooth.

❸ Scrape the dip into a bowl and garnish with chopped chives and remaining tablespoon of olive oil. Serve with toasted pita, vegetables, or olives if desired.

7

*Fresh 6-plant-part burritos, ready to roll.*

## Veggie Roll-Ups

Roll-ups make vegetables into tremendously kid-friendly finger foods. Older kids can help slice the veggies, and kids of all ages can select and arrange the veggies, spread the dip, and roll them up. Just about anything you have to harvest can work here. Nice raw options include beets, bell peppers, broccoli, carrots, cauliflower, cherry tomatoes, green beans, and snap or snow peas. You can also roast or sauté dark, leafy greens, eggplant, or potatoes.

**ACTIVE TIME:** *15 minutes*  **TOTAL TIME:** *15 minutes*
*Makes 18 sliced rolls*

**Here's what you'll need:**

> *Fresh vegetables from the garden*
> *6 large, whole grain tortillas*
> *Hummus, Baba Ganoush, Sunflower Seed*
>    *Green Bean Pâté, or any other spreadable*
>    *dip of choice*
> *Large frying pan*

**Here's what you'll do:**

**1** Harvest all of the veggies you want to use in your roll-ups. Slice larger items into strips, and grate root vegetables.

**2** Warm your tortillas on a hot frying pan to make them more pliable.

**3** Spread a layer of dip over your tortilla.

**4** Place veggies on the tortilla and roll it up. Be careful not to overstuff the tortilla with veggies to avoid cracking. Once rolled, slice into 2-Inch rolls, turn upright and serve.

**Also try this:**

If you are growing lettuce with big leaves, you can use a lettuce leaf in place of the tortilla. At Life Lab, kids love to make 6-plant-part burritos. We use lettuce leaves to wrap everything together, and help them place an edible root, stem, flower, fruit and seed inside (5 pieces inside plus the lettuce leaf wrap makes 6 plant parts). For example, they might have a piece of carrot, a piece of broccoli stem, a cauliflower floret, a cherry tomato, and a sugar snap pea inside. They roll these all up inside their lettuce leaves and eat them whole.

## Popcorn

Popcorn is a wonderful crop to grow with children. It grows fast and tall, creating a naturally cool, shady hideaway in the heat of the summer. The harvest window is long because it can dry on the stalk. And most kids love to prepare and eat popcorn.

**ACTIVE TIME:** *20 minutes*   **TOTAL TIME:** *20 minutes*
*Makes 2 quarts*

**Here's what you'll need:**

> *⅓ cup popcorn kernels*
> *1 air popper or large pot (at least 3-quart*
>    *capacity) with lid*
> *3 tablespoons canola, safflower, or grape-*
>    *seed oil, if using large pot*
> *Potholders, if using a large pot*

> *Topping ideas:*
> *2 tablespoons butter, melted*
> *Salt to taste*
> *chili powder, nutritional yeast, olive oil,*
>    *Parmesan cheese, soy sauce, sugar and*
>    *cinnamon*

**Here's what you'll do:**

**1** Harvest ears of popcorn when they are completely dry. If needed, store in a warm, indoor place until they dry completely.

**2** Have kids pick the corn off of the cob with their fingers into a bag or bowl. Starting a row of kernels yourself or breaking the cob

CONTINUED ⟶

## Curry Winter Squash Soup

If it grows in the summer, why is it called a winter squash? Winter squash is unique in the garden because it stores well, allowing us to enjoy its sweet flavor all the way through winter. It is also tremendously popular with kids because it's so sweet. This soup will make a wonderful, warm treat for you and your kids on a winter's day, when other garden produce is in limited supply. Older kids can chop and prepare vegetables, while kids of all ages can help you measure spices, scoop out the winter squash flesh, stir the soup, and use the blender.

ACTIVE TIME: *30 minutes*

TOTAL TIME: *1 hour, 15 minutes*

*Serves 4 as a main dish or 8 as a starter*

**Here's what you'll need:**

> 1 small edible pumpkin, medium-sized butternut, or other winter squash (or 20-ounce can of pumpkin puree)
> 3 tablespoons olive oil
> 1 leek, white part only, chopped
> 1 large yellow or white onion, peeled and chopped
> 4 cups vegetable broth
> ½ teaspoon salt
> ½ teaspoon curry powder
> ½ teaspoon nutmeg
> ¼ teaspoon ginger
> 1 bay leaf
> 1 cup coconut milk
> 1 bunch cilantro or chives, chopped (optional)
> Baking pan
> Large pot
> Food processor or blender

**Here's what you'll do:**

1. If roasting your own pumpkin or winter squash: preheat the oven to 350 degrees Fahrenheit. Cut the squash in half, scoop out and discard the seeds and strings, and poke the skin a few times with a fork. Rub 2 tablespoons of olive oil onto the cut edges and place cut edges down in a baking pan. Bake for about 45 minutes, until it's easy to push a fork into the flesh. Remove from the oven and cool, then scoop out the cooked squash and discard the skins.

2. Heat 1 tablespoon of olive oil in a large pot over medium heat. Add the chopped leek and onion and sauté until soft, about 10 minutes.

3. In a food processor or blender, puree the squash with the sautéed leek, onion, and vegetable broth. You may need to work in batches to get through all the squash.

4. Return the pureed squash mixture to the soup pot. Add the salt and spices. Bring to a boil over medium heat, stirring often, and then reduce the heat to low and simmer for about 15 minutes, uncovered. Stir occasionally.

5. Remove the bay leaf, add the coconut milk, and stir until the soup is hot.

6. Divide soup into bowls and serve garnished with chopped cilantro or chives.

## Garden Pizzas

Most kids love pizza, which makes it a great mechanism for encouraging them to try new vegetables. You can buy pre-made crust or make your own, using the recipe below. Regardless, involving your kids in topping the pizzas will make them more excited to taste their culinary creations. Older kids can chop and prepare vegetable toppings and kids of all ages can help you mix the dough ingredients, grate cheese, and add sauce, cheese, and other toppings to each pizza.

*Using too much sauce or other wet and heavy toppings will prevent the dough from becoming crisp, so remember that less is more when making pizza.*

ACTIVE TIME: *1 hour*  TOTAL TIME: *1 hour, 15 minutes*
*Makes 2 large rectangle sheets or 4 medium rounds*

### Here's what you'll need:

#### For the dough:
*4½ teaspoons (approximately 2 packages) active dry yeast*
*2⅔ cups warm water*
*7 to 7½ cups all-purpose flour, plus more for dusting work surface*
*7 tablespoons olive oil*
*2 tablespoons salt*
*2 tablespoons sugar*
*Coarse ground cornmeal (for dusting)*
*2 baking sheets or a round pizza stone*
*Rolling pin or other implement to roll out dough*
*Large mixing bowls*

There's nothing better than homemade pizza fresh from a wood fired-oven.

*Dish towels or plastic wrap*
***Topping ideas:***
*Tomato sauce or pesto sauce*
*Fresh produce, sliced or prepared: basil, bell peppers, fresh tomatoes, spinach, summer squash, zucchini, or others*
*Fresh produce, sliced and pre-cooked: asparagus, eggplant, leeks, potatoes, or others*
*Mozzarella cheese, grated*
*Fresh herbs*

### Here's what you'll do:
1 Combine the yeast, 1 tablespoon of sugar, and warm water in a large mixing bowl and let stand until the yeast is dissolved, about 5 minutes.

2 Add 4 tablespoons of olive oil, then flour, salt and remaining 1 tablespoon of sugar, and mix for about 1 minute CONTINUED →

⟶ GARDEN PIZZAS CONTINUED

to blend all of the ingredients.

**3** Knead for 10 to 15 minutes, until the dough is smooth and elastic. Divide dough and shape into 2 or 4 balls (depending on your baking method). Transfer each ball of dough to a mixing bowl, each greased with some of the remaining 2 tablespoons of olive oil. Turn each ball over once to coat.

**4** Preheat the oven to 475 degrees Fahrenheit. Place the baking sheets or pizza stone in the oven to preheat while you prepare the dough and toppings.

**5** One at a time, flatten the balls of dough on a lightly floured work surface and roll out into the desired shape.

**6** Remove baking sheets or pizza stone from the oven and dust lightly with cornmeal.

**7** Transfer the flattened dough to the pans. For pizza that will be heavily loaded, it's helpful to pre-bake the crust for 5 minutes before adding the sauce and other toppings.

**8** Spread your toppings of choice. Tomato sauce or pesto and mozzarella cheese are classic starters. From the garden, basil, bell peppers, fresh tomatoes, spinach, summer squash, and zucchini all make great additions. If you pre-cook them, asparagus, eggplant, leeks, and even potatoes are also delicious on pizzas.

**9** Bake for 10 minutes, or until desired crispness is achieved. Remove pans from oven, transfer pizzas to a cutting board and cut into slices or squares. Repeat with any remaining dough.

## Garden Frittatas

*A garden meal that's 100 percent fresh from the garden.*

What child doesn't love to crack an egg? If you and your family are raising chickens, your kids will also be thrilled to collect the eggs from under the hens. In this recipe, you will mix eggs with lots of fresh garden vegetables to create a delightful frittata for children and adults alike to enjoy. Older kids can prepare all of the ingredients, while children of all ages can help grate the cheese and crack and whisk the eggs.

**ACTIVE TIME:** *20 minutes* **TOTAL TIME:** *30 minutes*
*Serves approximately 6*

7

## Here's what you'll need:

*2 tablespoons olive oil*

*1 onion, peeled and chopped*

*2 leeks, white part only, chopped (optional)*

*4 cloves garlic, chopped*

*1 bunch leafy greens (kale, chard,*
*or collards), washed, stems and ribs*
*removed, and leaves chopped*

*2 small summer squash, sliced thin*

*¼ cup water*

*6 eggs*

*½ cup milk*

*¼ cup cheese, grated*

*1 tablespoon fresh oregano or ½ tablespoon*
*dried oregano*

*1 tablespoon fresh parsley, chopped*

*1 teaspoon salt*

*Pinch of pepper*

*1 large cast iron pan (if you don't have a cast*
*iron pan, you can cook this on the stove*
*in a regular frying pan and then transfer*
*to a casserole dish to finish in the oven)*

## Here's what you'll do:

**1** Preheat oven to 325 degrees Fahrenheit.

**2** Heat oil in a large cast iron or other type of frying pan over medium heat. Add chopped onions, leeks, and garlic and sauté for 3 minutes.

**3** Add greens, squash and water. Cover and cook over medium heat for 3 to 4 minutes.

**4** While the greens are cooking, whisk together in a separate bowl the eggs, milk, cheese, herbs, salt, and pepper.

**5** Add the egg mixture to the greens in the pan. Cover and cook over low heat until almost set, about 4 minutes.

**6** If cooking in a regular frying pan, transfer contents to casserole dish. Place the cast iron pan or casserole dish in the oven and bake for 5 to 8 minutes or until the frittata has browned lightly on top and is completely set in the center.

7

## Egg Drop Soup

Your kids will love to watch eggs turn into feathery wisps as you add them into this simple soup. You can vary the vegetables in this soup with whatever you have in season.

**ACTIVE TIME:** *20 minutes*  **TOTAL TIME:** *20 minutes*
*Makes 2 large or 4 small servings*

### Here's what you'll need:

> 2 leeks, diced
> 2 tablespoons olive oil
> 1 bunch chard or other dark, leafy greens, chopped
> 5 cups vegetable stock
> 2 eggs
> 2 tablespoons green onion or chives, chopped
> Salt and pepper to taste
> Soup pot

### Here's what you'll do:

**1** Sauté leeks with olive oil in your soup pot for 2 to 3 minutes.

**2** Add 1 cup of chopped chard and sauté for another 2 minutes.

**3** Add vegetable stock, bring to a boil, and cook until chard is tender and ready to eat, about 1 minute.

**4** Beat eggs in a small bowl and slowly pour into the boiling broth, stirring gently.

**5** Add salt, pepper, and green onions and serve hot.

## Zucchini Fritters

We love this recipe, not only for the delicious end result, but because kids of all ages can help with almost every step. This can be a fun cooking activity for a group, with one child grating zucchini, one grating lemon zest, one cracking and beating eggs, one measuring flour, oil, and salt, and one grating or crumbling cheese. Older children will also enjoy helping you flip the fritters on the pan.

**ACTIVE TIME:** *45 minutes*  **TOTAL TIME:** *45 minutes*
*Makes about 12 small fritters*

### Here's what you'll need:

> 1 pound (about 3 medium) zucchini
> ½ onion, diced
> 1 tablespoon of lemon zest, freshly grated
> 2 tablespoons fresh parsley, chopped
> 2 large eggs, lightly beaten
> ½ cup all-purpose flour
> ¼ cup Parmesan cheese, freshly grated, or feta cheese, crumbled
> 1 teaspoon salt
> Dash of freshly ground pepper
> 2 tablespoons canola oil, or more as needed
> Medium bowl
> Large frying pan

7

**Here's what you'll do:**

❶ In a medium bowl, coarsely grate the zucchini, leaving the skin on.

❷ Add diced onion, lemon zest, chopped parsley, eggs, salt, and pepper and mix well to combine.

❸ Slowly add the flour, stirring so no lumps form. Then fold in the cheese.

❹ Heat 2 tablespoons of oil in a large frying pan over medium-high heat. One at a time, carefully drop about 2 tablespoons of zucchini mixture into the hot pan; spacing fritters a few inches apart. Cook fritters until golden, 2 to 3 minutes. Reduce heat to medium. Flip fritters with a spatula, and continue cooking until golden on all sides, 2 to 3 minutes more.

❺ Transfer cooked fritters to a plate and set aside in a warm place. Repeat cooking process with any remaining zucchini mixture, adding more oil to pan if necessary.

## *Drinks*

## Green Garden Smoothie

Amy Carlson runs our garden field trips and summer camps at Life Lab, and is also mother to young daughter Greta. Between her work here and at home, Amy has loads of experience preparing garden-fresh foods with kids. Amy says she can think of no more effective way to "get raw, leafy greens into kids" than by incorporating them into fruit smoothies. In fact, by having one of these smoothies every morning, Amy has also dramatically increased her own consumption of dark, leafy greens. Greta helps Amy prepare the smoothies by chopping the leaves with her nylon knife and pushing the buttons on the blender.
*Drink right away or keep refrigerated for up to 24 hours.*
ACTIVE TIME: *15 minutes*  TOTAL TIME: *15 minutes*
*Makes 3 servings of 12 to 14 ounces*

**Here's what you'll need:**

  *1 bunch kale, spinach or chard, washed*
  *1 ⅓ cup water or juice*
  *¾ cup plain yogurt*
  *3–4 cups fresh and/or frozen fruit, chopped or sliced*
  *1–2 tablespoons nut butter (optional)*
  *1–2 tablespoons ground flax seed (optional)*
  *Blender*

CONTINUED ⟶

⟶ GREEN GARDEN SMOOTHIE CONTINUED

**Here's what you'll do:**

**❶** Remove stems from greens and coarsely chop or tear the leaves into pieces.

**❷** In a blender, combine the greens with 1 cup of water or juice until smooth, about 2 minutes.

**❸** Add yogurt, fruit, and nut butter and continue to blend until smooth. Add additional ⅓ cup of water or juice if needed to reach desired consistency.

**❹** If desired, stir in ground flax immediately before drinking.

**Also try this:**

• Change your smoothie with the seasons. For example, a great winter smoothie might include apple or pear (cored and sliced, with skin still on), citrus fruit (peeled, sectioned, and seeded), and frozen strawberries. Combining a tart-tasting fruit, such as berries or citrus, with milder fruits, such as apples or persimmons, complements the greens and yields a tasty smoothie.

• Experiment with other greens. Beet greens, escarole, and bok choy are all great in smoothies.

*After helping with the preparation, Greta enjoys her kale smoothie.*

*Tea time in the garden.*

## Herbal Tea

The most fun way to make herbal tea with kids is to heat water and carry it with you in a thermos while your kids gather and add the herbs of their choice. Follow this recipe to make tea while walking around the garden together. Good options for tea herbs include chamomile, lemon verbena, mint, and peppermint.

ACTIVE TIME: *5 minutes*   TOTAL TIME: *30 minutes*
*Makes up to 6 servings*

**Here's what you'll need:**

> Tea herbs growing in the garden
> 1 thermos
> Small tea cups
> Water

**Here's what you'll do:**

1. Boil a pot of water. Pour hot water into thermos.
2. Carry your full thermos with you as you and your kids take a walk around the garden.
3. Pick and rinse the herbs you want to include in your tea. Then throw them in, stem and all.
4. Let the tea brew for 5 minutes or more. Pour a little into a cup and check the temperature and flavor. When it feels and tastes right, serve and enjoy.

## Lemon Ice

This is a drink that could also be considered a dessert. It makes a deliciously refreshing treat on a warm day. Older kids can help with every step, and younger kids can help juice the lemons, measure sugar and lemon juice, and blend, garnish and serve the ices.

ACTIVE TIME: *15 minutes*   TOTAL TIME: *3 hours*
*Serves 7 to 9*

**Here's what you'll need:**

> 4 cups water
> 2 cups sugar
> 4 medium-sized lemons (or ¾ cup fresh
>    lemon juice)
> Saucepan
> Ice cube trays
> Food processor or blender

**Here's what you'll do:**

1. Place the water and sugar in a saucepan over medium-high heat. Boil for 5 minutes, stirring occasionally.
2. While the sugar water boils, slice lemons in half and juice them. Measure ¾ cup of lemon juice. Add lemon juice to sugar water and stir.
3. Remove the pot from the heat source and pour the mixture into ice cube trays. Freeze until solid.

CONTINUED →

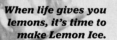

*When life gives you lemons, it's time to make Lemon Ice.*

⟶ LEMON ICE CONTINUED

**4** When you are ready to serve your lemon ices, pop the cubes from the tray into a food processor or blender and blend them very quickly. Make sure to stop before they melt.

**5** Spoon lemon ice into cups or bowls and serve with a straw and a spoon.

**Also try this:**

• Try these ices with other citrus fruits like oranges, limes, or grapefruit as they become ripe and available. You can also add mint or lemon verbena to the mixture before blending for a bolder, herbed flavor.

• Have your kids add garnishes to the ices: a mint or lemon balm leaf, or a slice of strawberry or lemon, for instance.

## Strawberry-Lime Spritzer

Sweet strawberries, tangy lime, and bubbly seltzer water make this drink a wonderful, healthy alternative to soda pop.

ACTIVE TIME: *45 minutes*

TOTAL TIME: *1 hour, 45 minutes*

*Makes about 15 servings*

### Here's what you'll need:

> *3 cups fresh or frozen strawberries, chopped*
> *1 cup sugar*
> *1 cup water*
> *⅓ cup lime juice*
> *1 ½ teaspoons lime zest*
> *Sparkling water*
> *Saucepan*
> *Blender*
> *Mesh strainer*

### Here's what you'll do:

1. Combine berries, sugar, water, and lime zest in a saucepan over medium heat and simmer until thickened, about 30 minutes.
2. Remove from heat and puree using blender.
3. Pour mixture through a fine mesh strainer into a bowl or jar, discarding the solids.
4. Stir in the lime juice and chill until cold.
5. To serve, pour about ¼ cup of strawberry-lime syrup into a glass and add sparkling water to taste. Stir and enjoy.

## Lemon-Rosemary Spritzer

Your friends and family will be happily surprised by this unique herbal combination.

ACTIVE TIME: *30 minutes*

TOTAL TIME: *1 hour, 30 minutes*

*Makes about 15 servings*

### Here's what you'll need:

> *1 cup lemon juice*
> *1 cup sugar*
> *½ cup water*
> *1 teaspoon fresh rosemary, finely chopped*
> *Sparkling water*
> *Saucepan*
> *Mesh strainer*

### Here's what you'll do:

1. Combine all of the ingredients in a saucepan over medium heat and simmer until slightly thickened, about 15 minutes.
2. Pour syrup through a fine mesh strainer into a bowl or jar, discarding the solids.
3. Chill until cold.
4. To serve, pour about ¼ cup of lemon-rosemary syrup into a glass and add sparkling water to taste. Stir and enjoy.

7

# Rhubarb Spritzer

Zowee! This is a delightfully sweet and sour drink.

*Be sure to remove and compost any rhubarb leaves; they are poisonous if ingested.*

**ACTIVE TIME:** *20 minutes*

**TOTAL TIME:** *1 hour, 20 minutes*

*Makes about 15 servings*

**Here's what you'll need:**

> 3 rhubarb stalks without leaves
> 2 cups water
> 1 cup sugar
> Sparkling water
> Small saucepan
> Slotted spoon

**Here's what you'll do:**

1. Wash and cut rhubarb stems into ¼-inch pieces.
2. Add rhubarb pieces to water in a small saucepan and bring to a simmer.
3. Simmer for 5 minutes to make a rhubarb syrup.
4. Strain out rhubarb pieces with slotted spoon. Add sugar and stir until it is fully dissolved.
5. Chill rhubarb syrup.
6. To serve, pour about ¼ cup of rhubarb syrup into a glass and add sparkling water to taste. Stir and enjoy.

Fresh fruit smoothies and spritzers are always a treat.

7

## Stewed Apples or Pears

When paired with something sweet, like ice cream or whipped cream, these stewed apples or pears make a wonderful dessert on a cold fall or winter day. Older kids can help by slicing the apples or pears, and kids of all ages can help you measure the apple juice, cinnamon, and salt; juice the orange; and grate the peel.

ACTIVE TIME: *30 minutes*   TOTAL TIME: *45 minutes*

*Serves 8 to12 as a dessert*

### Here's what you'll need:

*6 medium-sized apples or pears*
*1 medium-sized orange*
*1 cup apple juice*
*½ teaspoon cinnamon*
*¼ teaspoon salt*
*Saucepan*

### Here's what you'll do:

❶ Peel, core, and quarter the apples or pears.
❷ Zest and juice the orange.
❸ Place the apple or pear slices in a saucepan. Add the orange juice and zest, apple juice, cinnamon, and salt and bring to a boil over medium heat.
❹ Reduce the heat to low and simmer until the fruit is soft, 10–15 minutes.
❺ Serve in bowls plain or with yogurt, ice cream, whipped cream, or as a topping for pancakes.

## Strawberry-Rhubarb Tartlets

When kids come to Life Lab, we bring them to the rhubarb patch and cut off a leaf and stem. We compost the leaf (remember—rhubarb leaves are poisonous) and then chop the stem into bite-sized pieces and hand them out for our sour-face-making contest. After fair warning, all the kids who want to try something very sour take a bite and then watch one another react. We're not sure if this is more fun for the kids or the counselors. As you can imagine, it is hilarious. In this dessert, we sweeten the rhubarb with sugar and syrup and add strawberries for a delightful springtime treat.

ACTIVE TIME: *45 minutes*   TOTAL TIME: *45 minutes*

*Makes 4 tartlets*

### Here's what you'll need:

*6 graham crackers*
*4 teaspoons butter, melted*
*3 cups rhubarb, chopped*
*⅓ cup sugar*
*⅓ cup plus 1 teaspoon orange juice, divided and kept separate*
*Pinch of salt*
*1 teaspoon cornstarch*
*1 ½ cups strawberries, sliced*
*4 tablespoons cream cheese, softened*
*2 tablespoons vanilla yogurt*
*1 teaspoon maple syrup*
*Food processor or blender*
*4 tartlet pans*

CONTINUED →

7

*Just add sugar to make this sour stem sweet and tasty.*

**Here's what you'll do:**

1. To prepare crust, grind the graham crackers in a food processor or blender until fine. Add melted butter and continue to blend until combined, about 15 seconds more. Divide the crust equally between 4 tartlet pans, pressing the mixture into the bottom and up the sides of the pans. Set aside.

2. To prepare filling, combine rhubarb, sugar, ⅓ cup of orange juice, and salt in a saucepan. Cook over medium heat, stirring occasionally, until rhubarb is soft, about 10 minutes. In a small cup, combine the cornstarch with the remaining teaspoon of orange juice to dissolve and stir into the hot rhubarb mixture. Bring to boil over medium-high heat then reduce heat to low and simmer, cooking mixture for an additional 30 seconds, stirring frequently. Stir in strawberries and remove from heat. Divide among tartlet pans.

3. For topping, mix together the softened cream cheese, yogurt and maple syrup in a small bowl. Stir until smooth and spoon over the tartlets equally.

**Also try this:**

If you do not have tartlet pans, or just want to try an alternate technique, pour your rhubarb mixture into a large pie pan. Top with cream cheese topping and then crush the crust mixture over the top for a crumbly finish.

7

## Fresh Fruity Pops

Kids of all ages love popsicles. In this activity, they can use fresh garden produce to make their very own. Older kids can help slice the lemon and pour the mixture into cups, and kids of all ages can help blend the fruit, taste and sweeten the mixture, and put in the popsicle sticks.

ACTIVE TIME: *20 minutes*

TOTAL TIME: *4 hours, 20 minutes*

*Makes 12 popsicles*

### Here's what you'll need:

> *1 lemon*
> *1 basket of strawberries, either fresh*
>    *or semi-thawed*
> *Blender*
> *Pitcher*
> *Sugar to taste*
> *12 (3-ounce) paper cups*
> *Metal pan*
> *Popsicle sticks*

### Here's what you'll do:

1. Wash lemon, cut it in half, and squeeze the juice from one of the halves.
2. Wash and blend the berries.
3. Put the blended berries and lemon juice in a pitcher.
4. Add 2 cups of water and stir.
5. Add sugar to taste and stir again.
6. Set out paper cups in a metal pan.
7. Pour fruit mixture into cups and place the entire pan of cups in the freezer.
8. About 2 hours later, when the popsicles are frozen enough to hold a popsicle stick upright, push sticks into the center.
9. Leave the popsicles in the freezer for at least 2 more hours, or until they are frozen completely.

### Also try this:

These popsicles will work with almost any fresh fruit. Try different ones and choose your favorites. You can also experiment with adding yogurt to make creamier popsicles, or by sweetening with juice instead of sugar.

## Lavender-Lemon Shortbread Cookies

These delicious and simple shortbread cookies are an excellent complement to fresh herbal tea. Kids of all ages can help harvest the herbs, grate the lemon zest, remove and measure flowers from the lavender stalks, mix the ingredients, and press the dough into the pan.

**ACTIVE TIME:** *25 minutes*  **TOTAL TIME:** *1 hour*
*Makes about 12 cookies*

### Here's what you'll need:

> 1 cup unsalted butter, softened
> 1 cup sugar
> 2 teaspoons lemon verbena,
>     finely chopped, or lemon zest, grated
> 3 cups flour
> 2 teaspoons de-stemmed lavender flowers,
>     dried or fresh
> ¼ teaspoon salt
> Mixing bowls
> 8 × 8-inch baking pan or 9-inch pie pan

### Here's what you'll do:

1. Preheat the oven to 325 degrees Fahrenheit.
2. In a large mixing bowl, beat butter, sugar, and lemon verbena or lemon zest until creamy, 1 to 2 minutes.
3. In another bowl, mix together the flour, lavender, and salt. Add the flour mixture to the creamed butter mixture, stirring just until combined.

*Learning to use different kitchen tools keeps kids interested in cooking.*

4. Press the cookie dough into baking pan or pie pan. Pierce dough in a few places with a fork. To make cutting the cookies easier after baking, score the dough into equal squares or wedges with a knife, being careful not to cut completely through.
5. Bake until golden brown, 25–30 minutes. Let cool 5 minutes before cutting. Slice, remove from pan and enjoy.

*Learning to use a culinary knife is a skill kids will use their entire lives.*

## More Edible Activities

In addition to our seasonal cooking activities in Life Lab's Garden Classroom, there are a handful of edible activities that we like to do with whatever fruits or vegetables are in season at a given time of year.

### Farmers' Markets

If you and your kids have an abundance of any produce, it can be fun to set up a sale in your front yard. Label each item with the name and price. Even if you have too little produce to sell, it can be fun for young kids to set up a small farmers' market stand where their parents, grandparents, or other friends can come and role-play the farmers' market experience, purchasing, say, 10 green beans or three cherry tomatoes.

## Mmm, Mmm, Good—Comparative Tastings

A wonderful way to get your child eating new foods is to show a genuine interest in his or her opinion. For example, you might say, "Hey Luis. I'm making a salad tonight and I want to put sliced peaches on top. Which of these peaches do you think tastes sweeter? Which has the best texture?"

A comparative taste test provides a more structured way to gather kids' input on different varieties of the same crop. You might do this prior to selecting which variety of plum tree to plant, or which variety of winter squash to use in a soup. It is exciting for them to be able to contribute in this way. Taste tests also give us the opportunity to slow down and really experience the unique tastes within a garden crop. Finally, comparative taste tests can be fun with large groups, with each person casting a vote for his or her favorite.

To hold a taste test, have your kids harvest a single apple, for instance, from as many varieties as you have growing in the garden. You can also do this with produce from a farm, farmers' market, or grocery store. Help your kids wash and prepare each one for sampling. If you like, you can label each plate.

Then have your kids decide if they want to blindfold the participants or not. Have participants taste each variety and describe the unique textures and flavors to one another. Then have them decide which Malus domestica (apple) variety they like the best, and for which purposes. Maybe they will like 'Jonagold' best for salads, but 'Mutsu' for snacking. Your kids may want to take turns conducting and participating in the taste test. Allow them to blindfold you and serve you various apples as well.

Needless to say, this activity works well with all sorts of garden produce. At Life Lab, we conduct comparative taste tests on everything from winter squash to tomatoes. A local school even hosted a taste test with students to determine which foods to offer on their school lunch menu.

*Cream cheese snow on an evergreen tree.*

## Garden on a Cracker

This is a great activity for engaging your kids' creativity while also encouraging them to taste a wide variety of produce from the garden. Simply head out to the garden together and gather four or more fruits or vegetables that are edible when raw, and preferably are all different colors. You might grab a beet, a carrot, a yellow bell pepper, some broccoli, and some petals from a few edible flowers, for example. Grate carrots and beets, and chop all other veggies or fruits into bite-sized pieces. Then place each type of produce in a separate bowl.

Give your child a cracker and have them spread hummus, cream cheese, or another dip across the top. Now have them use the garden produce to create a miniature garden landscape on their cracker. They might put broccoli florets upright to represent trees, make a row of grated beets to mimic a brick pathway, or use a slice of yellow bell pepper as a miniature row of blooming sunflowers. Have them give you a tour of their garden and then enjoy their little garden snack.

7

*A neighbor's persimmons make a favorite dried fruit.*

**Chapter 8**

# PRESERVING THE HARVEST: from Fruit Leathers to Silly Dilly Beans

------------------------------

**SNEAK PEEK: Fruit leathers • Garlic braiding • Pickled pears • Ochoa's vanilla bean peach sauce • and more**

*Much of your garden's harvest can be frozen, canned, or dried.*

I t is difficult to think of anything that tastes better than an ear of corn, a cherry tomato, a peach, an apple, or any other fruit or vegetable picked and eaten right off of the plant. A very different taste sensation, however, that nearly rivals fresh fruit from the vine, is the taste of warm applesauce, roasted tomatoes, or peach preserves canned in the summer or fall and enjoyed in late winter. Perhaps because absence makes the heart grow fonder, or because anticipation is bottled right along with the harvest, you and your kids are sure to feel a small thrill when you twist the jar lid open and hear that signature "pop!" telling you that you have carried the summer forward—that you can take a short break from potatoes and winter squash, and enjoy a taste of summer on a cold winter's night.

Canning is not, of course, the only way to preserve food. By dehydrating, freezing, and braiding various crops, you can preserve them for months to come. And food is not the only garden treasure that you can preserve. Dried flowers and herbs can be used in balms, teas, wreaths, and more.

Our food preservation methods and recipes are organized from the simplest to the more complex. Regardless of which preserving methods you choose, kids of all ages will enjoy helping you prepare the preserves, and then waiting alongside you for that special day when you get to enjoy the final product.

## Freezing

You can freeze your garden produce to enjoy it long after the growing season has passed. To freeze produce, simply prepare it as you would for eating. For example, cut stems off of strawberries and slice them; blanch and chop broccoli, chard, or green beans; or prepare a potato leek soup. Remember, your items are easy to chop now, but they won't be once they're frozen solid, so do all of the slicing and chopping ahead of time. Then place your food in an airtight container, filling the container three-quarters full. For soups, sauces, and other fluid items, glass jars work well. For chopped or small produce, such as blueberries, zip-lock bags are great. If you are freezing something hot in a glass jar, leave it out to cool before placing it in the freezer.

Once frozen, some foods retain their quality better than others. Berries, sauces, and soups are all good bets. For more ideas of foods that freeze well, look through the frozen section of your grocery store. You'll see lots of frozen green beans, for example, but not many frozen tomatoes.

Food stored at 0 degrees Fahrenheit will remain safe indefinitely. The quality of frozen food, however, will slowly deteriorate. Therefore, we recommend eating your produce within 3 months of freezing it.

## Dehydrating

A dehydrator provides a very simple way to preserve many fruits and vegetables, and the change from a juicy apple or persimmon into a chewy dried fruit or fruit leather will prove both fascinating and educational for children. If you live in an area with hot, dry summers, you can use a store-bought or homemade solar food dehydrator. There are many do-it-yourself solar dehydration designs available online, such as those found at instructables.com/id/Solar-Food-Dehydrator-Dryer. This is a great option that makes use of salvaged building materials, conserves energy, and is free to use. For areas with moisture in the air year-round, however, an electric dehydrator will prove a good investment.

Once you have a dehydrator to use, older kids can help wash and slice the fruit you'll be drying. Apples, peaches, and persimmons are all nice options. Slice the fruits into $\frac{1}{8}$- to $\frac{1}{4}$-inch thick slices and dry until pliable and leathery. Drying times vary, and you can test out your fruit by tearing it. If moisture beads show up on the inside of the torn fruit, dry it some more. Store your dried fruit in an airtight jar or baggie.

If you or anyone you know has a 'Hachiya' persimmon (*Diospyrus kaki* 'Hachiya'), dehydrating is a particularly great option. This fruit is astringent until ripe and, once ripe, it is very, very soft. If you slice the unripe fruit, however, and dehydrate it, the dried product is deliciously sweet.

For a fun family activity, weigh your fruit before it is dehydrated and then make and record guesses about how much the dehydrated product will weigh. Then weigh the final product and compare this with your guesses. Was anyone close to guessing how much of the fruit's weight was made up of its water content?

## Fruit Leathers

Fruit leathers, or, as your kids may know them, fruit roll-ups, make wonderful, packable, healthy snacks year-round. Your kids will love turning freshly harvested fruit into mush, and then making that mush into fruit leathers. Apricots, apples, pears, berries, and plums are all great options to use.

ACTIVE TIME: *1 hour*   TOTAL TIME: *9–13 hours*
*Fills a 12 × 18-inch baking sheet. This can be cut into 9 strips of 2 × 12 inches, or into however many pieces you'd like.*

### Here's what you'll need:

*4 cups fresh fruit*
*¼ cup water*
*Sugar to taste*
*Lemon juice to taste*
*Saucepan*
*Potato masher*
*Baking pan*
*Parchment paper*

### Here's what you'll do:

1. Wash all fruit well and remove any stems, pits, seeds, or cores.
2. Chop all fruit. Now have a taste. If the fruit is tart, add a little sugar to taste. If it is already sweet enough, you can skip the sugar. If it is really sweet, add a bit of lemon juice.
3. Add all chopped fruit and ¼ cup of water to a saucepan and bring to a simmer. Cover and cook for 15 minutes, or until the fruit is cooked through, stirring occasionally.
4. Uncover the fruit and mash it up with a potato masher.
5. Cover a baking pan with parchment paper.
6. Spread a ⅛-inch layer of the fruit mixture evenly over the parchment paper.
7. Place the pan in the oven and heat the oven to 180 degrees. Cook for 8–12 hours, until the fruit leather is no longer sticky.

8

# Garlic Braiding

Together with your kids, braid the stems of soft-neck garlic bulbs to create a beautiful, decorative means for storing garlic from the garden. This is a particularly wonderful activity for any child who loves to braid their dolls' or friends' hair.

*Dried garlic should keep for a year.*

## HERE'S WHAT YOU'LL NEED:

12 heads of soft-neck garlic, harvested from the garden and sun-cured for at least 1 week

1 large kitchen knife or a pair of hand shears

2 (6-inch) pieces of twine

## HERE'S WHAT YOU'LL DO:

1 Harvest 12 heads of soft-neck garlic and cure them in the sun for at least 1 week, until they are completely dried out.

2 Clean your garlic bulbs. To do this, use your knife or shears to cut off the roots. Then remove the outermost layer of the bulb covering from each head of garlic.

3 Choose 3 heads of garlic that are about the same size and tie them together with a piece of twine.

4 Begin braiding the 3 stems. After you have finished your first braid, add 1 head of garlic, matching the stem with the middle stem. Now fold another strand over this one.

5 Now you have a new stem of garlic in the middle. Add another garlic stem to this strand. Continue braiding, adding a new stem to the center strand of the braid until all of the strands in the braid are made of 2 garlic stems, then 3, and finally 4.

6 Now braid the remaining strands up toward their tips. As you get close, use your second piece of twine to tie the stems together with a tight knot. Now tie in a loop of twine so that you have something from which to hang the braid.

7 Hang your garlic braid on your kitchen wall, or give it to a friend.

8 To use the garlic, just snip off a single garlic bulb at a time, close to the base of the stem. Once you have used all the bulbs, you can use the braided stems to spice up the hairdo on your scarecrow.

8

## Preserved Lemons

Kids will get a small lesson in the chemistry of food preservation as they preserve lemons by packing them in salt.

*This unique recipe will keep lemons for up to 6 months in the refrigerator without any need to boil your jars. The number of lemons you will use depends on their size, because you will put the lemons into the jar whole.*

ACTIVE TIME: *20 minutes*

TOTAL TIME: *2 weeks or longer*

*Makes 1 quart-sized jar*

### Here's what you'll need:

*One clean, quart-sized mason jar*
*2–4 lemons depending on size*
*Sea salt*
*Lemon juice (or additional lemons to juice)*

### Here's what you'll do:

1. Wash lemons and cut 4–6 evenly spaced slits running down the lemon rinds lengthwise. You want your knife to pierce the lemon rind to the flesh, but don't cut the lemon all the way through.

2. Squeeze the cut lemons slightly so that the slits open up just enough to stuff in salt. The salt cures the lemons and preserves them, so be generous with it.

3. When the lemons are packed with salt, put them in the mason jar and fill it with extra lemon juice to cover the lemons. You can pack the lemons in fairly tightly, squishing them down in the jar.

4. Place the jar in the refrigerator and label it with the date—the lemons will be preserved in 2 weeks and will last up to 6 months in the refrigerator. They will soften as they age, starting out fairly firm and ending up very soft.

5. When the lemons are preserved and you're ready to use them, simply slice them up, scoop out the insides, and cut the rinds into small pieces. The flavor is very strong, so you'll probably only use 1 lemon at a time. You can use the inside flesh in sauces or dressing, but most recipes call only for the rind. Preserved lemons add a wonderful flavor to chicken or fish dishes, couscous, or even salads.

8

## Pickled Pears

Give your pears a flavorful twist by pickling them. If you can the pickled pears, you'll be able to enjoy their delicious flavor long after the last pear has fallen from the tree.

ACTIVE TIME: *30 minutes*
TOTAL TIME: *40 minutes, plus time to process jars*
*Makes 10 half-cup servings*

### Here's what you'll need:

1 cup sugar
1 teaspoon whole cloves
2 cinnamon sticks
½-inch piece of fresh ginger
½ cup vinegar
½ cup water
1 medium lemon, sliced
6 firm, medium-sized pears
Large saucepan
Cheesecloth (optional)

### Here's what you'll do:

1 Peel, core, and cut your pears into quarters.
2 In a large saucepan, combine sugar, cloves, cinnamon, ginger, vinegar, water, and the sliced lemon. Stir well. If you'd like, you can wrap the cloves, cinnamon, lemon slices, and ginger in a piece of cheesecloth and put it into the water mixture like a teabag. If you don't mind navigating around a few whole cloves when you eat the pears, however, you don't need to bother.
3 Cook over medium heat until mixture comes to a boil. Then stir in the pears.
4 Cook over medium heat until pears are tender, but not falling apart, about 10 minutes. Remove cloves, cinnamon, lemon slices and ginger.
5 Transfer to a bowl, cover, and refrigerate for eating within the next few days, or can them to preserve for a later date.

8

## Silly Dilly Beans

These dilly beans really pack a punch—and a crunch. This is for families who like some spice, as the resulting dilly beans are full of flavor. Kids and adults both appreciate how they pop when you bite into them.

ACTIVE TIME: *1 hour*

TOTAL TIME: *1 hour, plus time to process cans*

*Makes about 8 pints*

### Here's what you'll need:

- 4 pounds green beans
- 5 cups white vinegar
- 5 cups water
- 7 tablespoons pickling salt
- 16 cloves garlic
- 2 teaspoons red pepper
- 16 slices serrano or jalapeño pepper
- 16 sprigs dill
- 1 teaspoon coriander
- 1 teaspoon caraway seeds
- 1 teaspoon mustard seeds
- Pitcher with spout
- 8 pint-sized jars

### Here's what you'll do:

1. Clean and sterilize your jars per the directions that came with your canner.
2. Mix white vinegar, water, and pickling salt in a pitcher with a spout. This is your brine.
3. Place 2 cloves garlic, ¼ teaspoon red pepper, 2 slices of serrano or jalapeño pepper, 1 dill head, and ⅛–¼ teaspoon each of coriander, caraway seeds, and mustard seeds into the bottom of each pint-sized jar. If you do this just after sterilizing the jars, the residual warmth allows the herbs to release a wonderful, savory smell.
4. Stick a tall green bean into a jar and then cut it so that it is just tall enough to stand in the jar vertically with an inch of headroom over it.
5. Use that bean as a measuring stick and cut all of the beans that same length.
6. Pack the green beans into each jar vertically, leaving 1 inch of headroom.
7. Fill each jar with brine, covering the beans and leaving ½ inch of headroom.
8. Use a rubber spatula to remove bubbles around the perimeter of the beans.
9. Follow the directions on your canner to process the cans.

### Also try this:

You can make Dilly Summer Squash using this same recipe. Simply slice zucchini or summer squash into spears and use in place of the green beans.

8

## Ochoa's Vanilla Bean Peach Sauce

Katy Pearce and her students at Anthony
W. Ochoa Middle School in Hayward, California,
mixed up this delicious creation last fall using
peaches from a tree in their school garden.
The flavor was sensational and now everyone
is waiting eagerly for the next harvest.
Enjoy your peach sauce on toast, in oatmeal,
or heated and spooned over ice cream.
*This delicious peach sauce can be refrigerated
for up to a month, or canned.*
ACTIVE TIME: *1 hour, 30 minutes* TOTAL TIME: *2 hours,
15 minutes, plus time to process jars*
*Makes 6–8 pints*

**Here's what you'll need:**

2 cups water
½ cup fresh squeezed lemon juice
Ice
8 pounds ripe peaches
2 cups sugar
1 large vanilla bean, split and seeded
1 large bowl
1 large pot

**Here's what you'll do:**

1. Combine water and lemon juice in a
   large pot.
2. Prepare an ice water bath in a large bowl or
   clean sink.
3. Bring another large pot of water to a boil.
   In small batches, blanch the peaches for 30
   seconds. Then plunge peaches into the ice
   water and drain. Repeat for all peaches.
4. Peel peaches. At this point, the skins should
   slip off. Remove the pits and slice peaches
   into rounds.
5. Add the peach slices and juices to the lemon
   juice and water.
6. Bring the peach mixture to a rolling boil,
   stirring often.
7. Add the sugar and scrape the vanilla bean
   seeds into the pot. Stir.
8. Lower the heat, simmering until the
   sauce is thickened to desired consistency,
   approximately 30–45 minutes.
9. Refrigerate the peach sauce or can the
   mixture.

8

Fresh offerings from a garden salad party.

# Chapter 9

## Let the Festivities Begin:

# GARDEN CELEBRATIONS

**SNEAK PEEK: Little sprouts soiree • Honeybee birthday party • National Leave-a-Zucchini-on-Your-Neighbor's-Porch Day • Garden party favors • and more**

Yards and gardens make great party settings, even for Alaskan pirates.

**C**elebrating the fruits of our labor is a common joy shared by families that garden. Garden fairy parties, flashlight garden scavenger hunt sleepovers, and honeybee-themed birthdays are all examples of ways families weave the garden into their events and parties.

Holidays and birthdays are on an annual cycle that helps shape family traditions and celebrations. The garden works the same way. If we look at the cycle of a garden and the seasons that drive that cycle, there are more reasons to celebrate than we could likely fit into our lives. From pulling well-kept carrots from under the snow for Thanksgiving in Alaska, to canning dilly beans in the middle of the summer to give to Grandma, many of the families we spoke with mentioned traditions tied to the garden that focus on reaping the harvest.

## A Reason to Party– Seasonal Themes

Making pie, sauce, and cider, and having bobbing contests are all great ways to celebrate the apple harvest. Whether you have your own apple

9

tree or you get apples from a u-pick orchard or farmers' market, your family can create seasonal harvest traditions around this wonderful fruit. And apples are only an example—you can celebrate any garden crop when it is abundant. Spotting the first flowering bulb of the winter, harvesting potatoes, or roasting sweet corn are all great excuses to gather friends, eat together, and celebrate.

The list of what families do together to celebrate their harvests could fill its own book. Here are some brilliant examples of seasonal party theme ideas that family gardeners shared with us.

## Summer

### Firefly Campfire
Prepare a nighttime flashlight-led scavenger hunt around the garden, and then gather around a fire pit for roasted corn.

### Bug Party
Make insect collecting nets and use bug boxes to collect bugs. Have a bug race. If you dare, serve chocolate covered insects.

### Water Party
Paint metal watering cans, set up a slip and slide or sprinklers to play in, and have a water balloon toss.

### Community Jam
Canning and jamming are not quick and easy tasks, which is all the more reason to include the whole family or neighborhood. Have the little ones harvest and wash produce and older kids can help slice and can.

## Fall

### Floral Fiesta
Make floral wreaths and other crafts, such as mini dried bouquets and dried pepper ristras.

### Seed Social
Collect seeds for saving, roast sunflower seeds, pop popcorn, make seed mosaics.

### Harvest Festival
Make cornhusk dolls, eat a garden bounty meal, make a stone soup, carve pumpkins and roast their seeds, make apple pie and press cider.

## Winter

### Garden Stones
Make stepping stones, paint stone plant markers, and make hypertufa planter pots.

### Bird Connections
Make birdseed wreaths, homemade bird feeders, suet cakes; collect nest building materials to set out in an onion bag for birds to collect; go bird watching; set up a bird blind.

## Spring

### Salad Party
Harvest a salad from your garden, or have friends bring ingredients to make a potluck salad. At the party, sow lettuce seeds in paper pots.

### Little Sprouts Soiree
Host a seed-sowing party. Make root-view cups for planting, and serve sprouted greens, nuts, and other seedy snacks in little cups.

### Wild Greens Party
Harvest wild greens, like miner's lettuce, to make a salad, and dandelion greens to make tea.

9

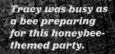
*Tracy was busy as a bee preparing for this honeybee-themed party.*

## Garden-Themed Birthdays

Garden-themed parties are limited only by your imagination. At Raine's 5th birthday party, her mother, Tracy, set up a project where kids bundled up 8-inch pieces of bamboo with rubber bands to make solitary beehives. Tracy had little instruction labels on how to install their hives at home and the kids used rubber stamps to decorate them. Other activities included tasting honey, pollen, and honey in the comb. In addition to mini bee homes, they also took home honey sticks, bee stickers, and honey taffy as party favors. The bee-themed garden party was capped off with a beehive cake. Tracy had another garden-themed party for her son's 4th birthday. Kids went home with 5-inch terra-cotta

Seed mosaics are fun for partygoers of all ages.

pots with baby ball carrots growing in them and bug boxes with live lady bugs inside.

For Neli's garden birthday, we set up stations for partygoers. Flowers were snipped and strung on strings to make flower "bling" (necklaces). Popcorn grown the prior year was out for kids to pick off the cob and air pop. A seed-sowing station with sunflower seeds and empty planter pots served as do-it-yourself party favors. And the favorite of all activities was the mud sculpture station where kids mixed soil and water in buckets and then sculpted art on cardboard pallets. The day ended with fresh peach pie and hand-cranked ice cream.

At Greta's birthday celebration, which took place on a chilly, fog-covered morning,

## National Leave-a-Zucchini-on-YOUR-Neighbor's-PORCH Day

WHY NOT MAKE up your own national garden holidays? This zucchini day idea was shared by a friend of ours who had the urge to anonymously distribute her overabundance of summer squash. A related idea was shared by another family that hosts a How Many Ways Can You Cook a Zucchini? party where friends bring summer squash dishes. If only we could get these creative minds together, we might start a zucchini revolution.

9

245

*Water play is even more fun at a birthday party.* •
*A group of gamesters twist it up playing human knot.*

partygoers created crafts to take home, such as lavender sachets and seed mosaics. Clippers, hot water, and mugs were available for harvesting herbal tea from the garden, and a fir pit was lit to keep folks warm. Chickens were fed and pet, and the mulberry tree was picked over. Garden veggie snacks, such as sweet pepper slices and apples, were followed by a cake dusted with powdered sugar flower imprints.

## Other Ideas for Garden-Themed Parties

Most kids' birthdays include an invitation, games or activities, food, and party favors. The garden can be incorporated into some or all of these aspects of a party, regardless of the time of year. Here are some ideas for every step, from planning to party day.

### Invitations

If you plan to send out invitations, infuse them with a garden motif. Make or purchase paper with embedded seeds for a plantable announcement. Seed packets made from coin envelopes, or envelopes you fold yourself, can carry the party details on the outside with something to sow on the inside.

### Activities

Create a craft project that is fun, educational, and gives the kids a sense of ownership, such as painting pots and planting succulent cuttings in them. You can find a list of activities we suggest for parties—even if it happens to be cold or rainy that day—at the back of this book.

*Edible projects engage partygoers, and feed them too.*

## Group Games

Even without introducing a game to play, kids left out in a yard usually come up with one of their own. Three-legged, potato sack, and wheelbarrow races are classic outdoor games. Other classics include limbo, jump rope, and water balloon tossing. Water games are especially fun in a summer garden, and just turning on the sprinklers can make for many smiles. Water relays, where kids pass a cup of water above their head to fill a bucket on the end of a line allows kids to play with water without getting quite as drenched as they will under sprinklers.

Tail tag is one of our favorites. Each kid has a tail made from a piece of cloth stuck in the back of his or her waistband. While the kids are in a defined area marked off by a garden hose or long rope, they try to pull out each other's tails. If they lose their tail, they go to the outside of the boundary and try to pull tails from the outside. The last person with an intact tail wins.

Most kids know how to play freeze tag. If you are tagged, you have to freeze with your feet spread wide. Players that are frozen can be freed to run if another player crawls under their legs. It is semi-organized chaos, but kids like it. Elbow tag and sharks and minnows are fun as well, and get young bodies moving. If you don't know how to play those, just ask a kid.

## Party Favors

Garden-themed take-home gifts are plentiful, and always appreciated. Bug boxes, little hand tools, hand lenses, seeds, and baby plants all come to mind. We hope we've also given you plenty of ideas in this book for activities in which kids make things they can take home, like milk carton birdhouses, planet-friendly paper pots, leaf press candles, or rock plant labels.

## Garden-Themed Food

Have you ever eaten a compost cake? Layers of crumbled cookies and ice cream are sprinkled with caramel, and gummi worms climb out the sides. Foods that kids help make are also very popular. Hand-pressed tortillas are a great addition to a taco or quesadilla bar. Top-your-own mini garden pizzas, where kids pick and prep their own toppings, are always well received. And, of course, we hope this book has given you lots of recipe ideas that are easy to incorporate into party plans.

9

# FAVORITE ACTIVITIES

## FOR

## Specific Situations

In a hurry to find the right activity or recipe
for the situation? Here is a quick-reference guide
with some of our favorites.

## Best Activities and Recipes for Toddlers

## Best Activities and Recipes for Teens

## Best Quick and Easy Activities and Recipes

## Websites

**lifelab.org**: Educational, garden-based activities, songs, recipes and more.

**kidsgardening.org**: A one-stop resource for school gardening, family gardening, grants, and other resources by the National Gardening Association.

**communitygarden.org**: Find community gardens in your region.

## Family Garden Activities

Cohen, Whitney, and Life Lab. 2010. *Kids' Garden: 40 Indoor and Outdoor Activities and Games.* Cambridge, MA: Barefoot Books.

Denee, Joanne, with Jack Peduzzi and Julia Hand. 1996. *In the Three Sisters Garden: Native American Stories and Seasonal Activities for the Curious Child.* Dubuque, IA: Kendall/Hunt Publishing.

Editors of Klutz. 2010. *Good Growing: A Kid's Guide to Green Gardening.* Palo Alto, CA: Klutz Press.

Gladstar, Rosemary. 2001. *Rosemary Gladstar's Family Herbal: A Guide to Living Life with Energy, Health, and Vitality.* North Adams, MA: Storey Publishing.

Hanneman, Monika, Patricia Hulse, Brian Johnson, Barbara Kurland, and Tracey Patterson. 2007. *Gardening with Children.* New York, NY: Brooklyn Botanic Garden.

Jaffe, Roberta, and Gary Appel. 2007. *The Growing Classroom: Garden-Based Science.* 2nd ed. South Burlington, VT: National Gardening Association.

Life Lab. 2010. *Sowing the Seeds of Wonder: Discovering the Garden in Early Childhood Education.* South Burlington, VT: National Gardening Association.

Lovejoy, Sharon. 1999. *Roots, Shoots, Buckets and Boots: Gardening Together with Children.* New York, NY: Workman Publishing.

Lovejoy, Sharon. 2001. *Sunflower Houses: A Book for Children and Their Grown-Ups.* New York, NY: Workman Publishing.

Lovejoy, Sharon. 2009. *Toad Cottages and Shooting Stars: Grandma's Bag of Tricks.* New York, NY: Workman Publishing.

McCorquodale, Elizabeth. 2010. *Kids in the Garden: Growing Plants for Food and Fun.* London: Black Dog Publishing.

Parrella, Deborah. 1995. *Shelburn Farms Project Seasons: Hands-On Projects for Discovering the Wonders of the World.* Shelburn, VT: The Stewardship Institute.

Woram, Catherine, and Martyn Cox. 2008. *Gardening with Kids.* London: Ryland Peters & Small.

## Children and Nature

Cornell, Joseph. 1979. *Sharing Nature with Children.* Nevada City, CA: Dawn Publications. Revised and updated, 1998.

Koontz, Robin. 1998. *The Complete Backyard Nature Activity Book.* New York, NY: Learning Triangle Press.

Lingelbach, Jenepher. 1986. *Hands-On Nature: Information and Activities for Exploring the Environment with Children.* Woodstock, VT: Vermont Institute of Natural Science.

Louv, Richard. 2006. *Last Child in the Woods: Saving our Children from Nature-Deficit Disorder.* Chapel Hill, NC: Algonquin Books.

Skelsey, Alice, and Gloria Huckaby. 1973. *Growing Up Green: Parents and Children Gardening Together.* New York, NY: Workman Publishing.

Sobel, David. 1999. *Beyond Ecophobia: Reclaiming the Heart in Nature Education.* Great Barrington, MA: Orion Society.

## Garden Design for Children

Danks, Sharon. 2011. *Asphalt to Ecosystems: Design Ideas for Schoolyard Transformation.* Oakland, CA: New Village Press.

Dannenmaier, Molly. 2008. *A Child's Garden: 60 Ideas to Make Any Garden Come Alive for Children.* Portland, OR: Timber Press.

Guinness, Bunny. 1996. *Creating a Family Garden: Magical Outdoor Spaces for All Ages.* New York, NY: Abbeville Press.

Hastings, Chris. 1997. *The Zoo Garden: 40 Animal-Named Plants Kids Can Grow Themselves*. Marietta, GA: Longstreet Press.

Kashef, Ziba. 2008. *Backyards for Kids: Playhouses, Sandboxes, Tree Forts, Swing Sets, Sports Areas and More.* Des Moines, IA: Oxmoor House Books.

Krezel, Cindy. 2008. *101 Kid-Friendly Plants: Fun Plants and Family Garden Projects.* West Chicago, IL: Ball Publishing.

Leendertz, Lia. 2008. *Family Garden*. New York, NY: Dorling Kindersley Publishing.

Matthew, Clare, and Clive Nichols. 2005. *Great Gardens for Kids.* 2nd ed. London: Hamlyn.

Moore, Robin. 1993. *Plants for Play: A Plant Selection Guide for Children's Outdoor Environments.* Berkeley, CA: MIG Communications.

## Edible Gardening

Barbarow, Peter. 1990. *Give Peas a Chance: Organic Gardening Cartoon-Science.* Happy Camp, CA: Naturegraph Publishers.

Brennan, Georgeanne, and Ethel Brennan. 1997. *The Children's Kitchen Garden: A Book of Gardening, Cooking, and Learning.* Berkeley, CA: Ten Speed Press.

Eierman, Colby. 2012. *Fruit Trees in Small Spaces: Abundant Harvests from Your Own Backyard.* Portland, OR: Timber Press.

Jeavons, John. 1991. *How to Grow More Vegetables Than You Ever Thought Possible on Less Land Than You Can Imagine.* Berkeley, CA: Ten Speed Press.

Katzen, Mollie. 2005. *Salad People and More Real Recipes: A New Cookbook for Preschoolers and Up.* New York, NY: Tricycle Press.

Liebreich, Karen, Jutta Wagner, and Annette Wendland. 2009. *The Family Kitchen Garden: How to Plant, Grow and Cook Together.* Portland, OR: Timber Press.

Taylor, Lisa, and the Gardeners of Seattle Tilth. 2011. *Your Farm in the City: An Urban-Dweller's Guide to Growing Food and Raising Animals.* New York, NY: Blackdog and Leventhal.

Toensmeier, Eric. 2007. *Perennial Vegetables: From Artichokes to Zuiki Taro, A Gardener's Guide to Over 100 Delicious and Easy to Grow Edibles.* White River Junction, VT: Chelsea Green Publishing.

## Children's Books

Asch, Frank. 2008. *The Earth and I.* New York, NY: Sandpiper.

Barry, Frances. 2008. *Big Yellow Sunflower.* Somerville, MA: Candlewick.

Brown, Ruth. 2001. *Ten Seeds.* Atlanta, GA: Anderson Press.

Carle, Eric. 1987. *The Tiny Seed.* New York, NY: Little Simon.

Cherry, Lynne. 2003. *How Groundhog's Garden Grew.* New York, NY: Blue Sky Press.

Cooney, Barbara. 1985. *Miss Rumphius.* New York, NY: Puffin.

Ehlert, Lois. 1991. *Growing a Vegetable Soup.* New York, NY: Sandpiper Press.

Ehlert, Lois. 1992. *Planting a Rainbow.* Boston, MA: Hartcourt Brace.

Fleishman, Paul. 2004. *Seedfolks.* New York, NY: Harper Trophy.

Fleishman, Paul. 2002. *Weslandia.* Somerville, MA: Candlewick.

Glaser, Omri. 2000. *Round the Garden.* New York, NY: Harry N. Abrams.

Hoberman, Mary Ann. 2004. *Whose Garden Is It?* Boston, MA: Hartcourt Childrens Books.

Lin, Grace. 2009. *The Ugly Vegetables.* Watertown, MA: Charlesbridge Publishing.

Mazer, Ann. 1991. *The Salamander Room.* New York, NY: Alfred A. Knopf.

Mockford, Caroline. 2007. *What's This? A Seed's Story.* Cambridge, MA: Barefoot Books.

Peck, Jan, and Barry Root. 1998. *The Giant Carrot.* New York, NY: Dial Books for Young Readers.

Stevens, Janet. 1995. *Tops and Bottoms.* Boston, MA: Hartcourt Childrens' Books.

Tierra, Leslie. 2010. *A Kid's Herb Book: For Children of All Ages,* Bandon, OR: Robert Reed Publishers.

# Metric Conversions

| INCHES | CENTIMETERS |
|---|---|
| $\frac{1}{4}$ | 0.6 |
| $\frac{1}{2}$ | 1.3 |
| $\frac{3}{4}$ | 1.9 |
| 1 | 2.5 |
| 2 | 5.1 |
| 3 | 7.6 |
| 4 | 10 |
| 5 | 13 |
| 6 | 15 |
| 7 | 18 |
| 8 | 20 |
| 9 | 23 |
| 10 | 25 |

| FEET | METERS |
|---|---|
| 1 | 0.3 |
| 2 | 0.6 |
| 3 | 0.9 |
| 4 | 1.2 |
| 5 | 1.5 |
| 6 | 1.8 |
| 7 | 2.1 |
| 8 | 2.4 |
| 9 | 2.7 |
| 10 | 3 |
| 20 | 6 |
| 30 | 9 |
| 40 | 12 |

## DRY VOLUME MEASUREMENTS

| | |
|---|---|
| $\frac{1}{8}$ teaspoon | 0.5 mL |
| $\frac{1}{4}$ teaspoon | 1 mL |
| $\frac{1}{2}$ teaspoon | 2 mL |
| $\frac{3}{4}$ teaspoon | 4 mL |
| 1 teaspoon | 5 mL |
| 1 tablespoon | 15 mL |
| 2 tablespoons | 30 mL |
| $\frac{1}{4}$ cup | 60 mL |
| $\frac{1}{3}$ cup | 75 mL |
| $\frac{1}{2}$ cup | 125 mL |
| $\frac{3}{4}$ cup | 175 mL |
| 1 cup | 250 mL |
| 2 cups | 500 mL |
| 3 cups | 750 mL |
| 4 cups | 1 L |

## TEMPERATURES

Degrees Fahrenheit
$(\frac{9}{5} \times$ degrees Celsius$) + 32$

## FLUID VOLUME MEASUREMENTS

| | |
|---|---|
| 1 ounce | 30 mL |
| 4 ounces | 125 mL |
| 8 ounces | 250 mL |
| 12 ounces | 375 mL |
| 16 ounces | 500 mL |
| 1 pint | 500 mL |
| 1 quart | 1 L |
| 1 gallon | 4 L |

# Photo Credits

Abby Bell: 12 (right), 100 (left), 116, 122, 128, 130, 134, 209, 211, 224, 225

Sarah Berkowitz: 12 (left)

Amy Carlson: 126, 216

Dave Carlson: 234 (bottom right)

Caitlin Clark: 233

Whitney Cohen: 13 (left), 16, 21, 22 (right), 30 (left), 31, 33 (right), 37 (top right), 40, 41, 44, 47, 52, 54, 55, 56, 71, 72 (top), 93, 99, 100 (right), 106, 110, 114, 135, 155, 163 (left), 176, 184, 187, 195, 198, 203, 204, 205, 220

Sharon Danks: 26, 28, 32, 58, 119, 124, 218

Alicia Dickerson: 13 (right), 83 (bottom), 92 (bottom), 101 (top), 112, 144, 146, 150, 153, 175, 178, 240, 246 (bottom)

John Fisher: 18, 22 (left), 25 (bottom left, right), 30 (top right, bottom right), 33 (left), 34, 35, 36, 37 (left, bottom right) 38, 39, 45, 50, 62, 65, 68, 72 (bottom), 73, 75, 76, 77, 78, 79, 80, 82, 83 (top 4), 85, 87, 89 (right), 90 (bottom), 91, 92 (top), 94, 98, 100, 101 (bottom), 102, 104, 113, 120, 131, 132, 133, 136, 137, 138, 139, 162, 163 (right), 165, 166, 168, 174, 180, 182, 186, 189, 191, 192, 197, 200, 206, 212, 217, 228, 234 (top left), 235, 245, 246 (top)

Helen Golden: 14 (bottom)

Nadine Golden: 35 (bottom), 265

Laurel Granados: 66

Tod Haddow: 14 (top), 95, 147, 148, 188, 265

Gail Harlamoff: 222

Elizabeth Ann Hill: 194, 196

Daniella Irish: 121, 164, 227, 230, 247

Matthew Levesque: 42

Tracy Matthes: 244

Kris Nemeth: 25 (top left), 170, 242

Erica Perloff: 10

Stacy Scheel: 140

Paul Simon: 88, 89 (left)

Stacey Stagliano: 24

Rachel VanLaanen: 35 (top), 90 (top)

# Index

# About the Authors

**Whitney Cohen** is the education director at Life Lab, a nationally recognized organization that teaches people to care for themselves, each other, and the world through farm- and garden-based programs. Guided by her joy in being outdoors with children, she is the author of the award-winning *Kids' Garden* activity card set and a contributor to other garden-based learning activity guides. She presents hands-on garden education workshops to varied audiences, including schoolteachers, parents, college students, food service directors, and Master Gardeners across the country. Her expertise in gardening with children comes from years as an environmental educator, a middle school science teacher, a teacher trainer, and, most recently, a mother. Whitney and her husband, Tod, love nothing more than spending time outdoors with their son, Nation.

**John Fisher** has worked as a garden-based educator for most of his adult life, sharing teachable moments in the garden with thousands of children and adults. John helped design and managed Life Lab's 1-acre Garden Classroom site, has contributed to a multitude of garden-based curricula, and has created videos and websites on garden-based learning, both at Life Lab and at the University of California Santa Cruz Farm. His first memorable gardening experience was as a child, harvesting cucumbers and tomatoes in his grandfather's garden. With his wife, Nadine, and young son, Neli, John tends a small suburban garden plot of 15 dwarf fruit trees, mixed berries, vegetable and cut flower gardens, and a small flock of friendly hens, in Santa Cruz, California. Seeing his son searching for the ripest berries and feeding snails to their hens puts a smile on John's face.

2 1982 03026 0826